£6-75+

Humanism in Adversity

Humanism in Adversity

TEACHERS' EXPERIENCE OF INTEGRATED HUMANITIES IN THE 1980s

Edited by
Douglas Holly

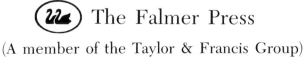 The Falmer Press

(A member of the Taylor & Francis Group)
London and Philadelphia

32433

UK	The Falmer Press, Falmer House, Barcombe, Lewes, East Sussex, BN8 5DL
USA	The Falmer Press, Taylor & Francis Inc., 242 Cherry Street, Philadelphia, PA 19106-1906

First published 1986

Library of Congress Cataloging in Publication Data

Humanism in adversity.

Includes index.
1. Education, Humanistic—England—Leicestershire.
2. Interdisciplinary approach in education—England—Leicestershire. 3. Education, Secondary—England—Leicestershire—Curricula. I. Holly, Douglas.
LC1011.H814 1986 001.3′07′124254 86-4595
ISBN 1-85000-100-6
ISBN 1-85000-101-4 (pbk.)

Typeset in 11/13 Caledonia by
Imago Publishing Ltd, Thame, Oxon.

Printed in Great Britain by Taylor & Francis (Printers) Ltd, Basingstoke

Contents

Foreword   vii

General Introduction — on Humanistic Learning   1
Douglas Holly

Why Integrate?   9
John Haslam

The Role of Language Support   22
Viv Styles

Developing a True Integrated Humanities Syllabus   31
Ross Phillips

The Story of a Syllabus   39
Lesley King

The Process Model of Integrated Humanities:
Some Principles of Work in the Early Secondary Years   53
Jim Greany and Derek Francis

Oral History in Integrated Humanities   63
Carol Saunders

Integrated Humanities in the Inner City School   76
G. A. Coleby

Patriarchy, Ethnocentrism and Integration   83
Carolyn Robson

Strategies for Curriculum Change: How to Implement an
Integrated Humanities Course   94
Den Corrall

Content

Geography and Integration   107
Vivien Keller

English and Integration: Some Problems of Intent   122
Jeff Lancaster

The Integrated Humanities Association:
Some Recent History   135
Deirdre Smith

Notes on Contributors   144

Foreword

This volume — with the exception of its editor's efforts — is the work of practising teachers. Nearly all have some connection with Leicestershire — for two reasons: Leicestershire is the local authority area I am most involved with as a teacher-trainer; also it is the area where there is more concentration of integrated practice than anywhere in the country.

It is a mistake made by too many people that educational practitioners are concerned only with the nuts and bolts, theory being for Schools of Education. I hope this collection will help to dispel that illusion. Integrated humanities as a practice is *about* theory: since it is not a 'discipline of knowledge' its practitioners can take nothing theoretical for granted. Daily they are called upon to expound on 'What it's all about? — to colleagues, superiors, parents, visitors and, not least, their own students. Few expect this of physicists, PE teachers or geographers. In one sense this continuous inquisition has been healthy: it has kept those who teach integrated humanities on constant intellectual alert, so to speak. But it can also be tiring, and a little dispiriting. I hope that from now on those who question the validity or the intellectual credentials of the approach will be directed to this volume — not as the last word but as one of the first. It is high time that so much energy, determination and sheer mental doggedness was rewarded by wider recognition, both in the halls of academe — by now somewhat dilapidated — and among a wider public. If the volume achieves anything in that direction its authors will be well satisfied.

Doug Holly
University of Leicester School of Education
December 1985

General Introduction — on Humanistic Learning

Douglas Holly

Human history is a puzzling thing — full of paradoxes and contradictions. And nothing, surely, can be more paradoxical than what is reported in this book: an expansionist educational policy being pursued in the teeth of continuing economic decline. With public expenditure in schools, as everywhere else, being severely pruned it seems amazing that new and vital approaches are being adopted by teachers in the curriculum area most threatened with curtailment — the humanities. But this paradox, like all paradoxes is only an *apparent* contradiction. It is the very severity of the threat which is forcing the pace of a development that began in less troubled times. Necessity is, as ever, the mother of invention.

Much of what the following chapters discuss will not come as a completely new revelation to many readers — integrated humanities in one form or another has been engaged in by secondary schools in many parts of the country for twenty years now. What perhaps *is* different is the degree of refinement in the theory and practice which some of the accounts reveal — the outcome of the historical circumstance that this practice has tended to be more concentrated in Leicestershire than anywhere else. It is important to emphasize this point, so that the collection will not be misinterpreted by other practitioners in other parts of the country. None of the contributors would claim that what they are doing has some special virtue or is necessarily different or better than the practice of colleagues elsewhere. But while integrated humanities practice in other parts of the country has frequently been isolated, the concentration of such practice in one relatively small area has allowed teachers to meet and confer — often informally and in their own time — to the extent that both theory and practice have inevitably been sharpened up. The reflections in this book are the result of that process.

1

The collection, in fact, grew out of a DES regional course held in Leicestershire in October 1984, when many of the contributors acted as discussion leaders. The theme then was 'Integrated Humanities in the Core Curriculum', and this is the essential 'message' of this book — that integration should be seen, not as some peripheral experiment with the curriculum, but as a *central* concern for teachers in an area under threat. The health of humanities — and even its very existence in a form which teachers would wish to see — may well lie in a fundamental rethinking of this part of the curriculum. So those currently involved in revitalizing the humanities are making history in circumstances decidedly not of their own choosing, and in a growing number of cases are doing it precisely *because* of adversity. The move towards integration in this and other areas of the curriculum may be characterized by sceptics as 'opportunism'. It is better understood as 'pragmatism'. The difference is basic: opportunism makes use of circumstances to advance selfish ends, pragmatism reacts to circumstances by turning them to the general advantage. The theme of pragmatism recurs constantly in the various contributions — it is one of the linking themes. It represents the positive reaction of principled realists.

To say, then, that the current upturn in the fortunes of an integrationist philosophy is the result of falling rolls is not at all, as its detractors suppose, to condemn the process but, on the contrary, to *commend* it. To make a positive out of a negative may be difficult in the abstract logic of mathematics — in human affairs it is common-place, and the origin of much of what we know as progress. At a time when public expenditure on education is being continuously reduced and the relevance of non-vocational education questioned in the highest quarters, the first casualty may soon be any experience by the majority of young people of constituent subjects in the humanities. In these circumstances the proper response should not be to drop history, say, as an area of study or to make it available only to some minority — probably an elite minority — but to have it taught by a *team*, most of whom are not history specialists, as an essential part of an integral area of experience. Integrated humanities without a historical dimension is, quite simply, *not* integrated humanities. Nor as a matter of fact, can integrated humanities be imagined without a knowledge of geographical interrelatedness, a spiritual/moral dimension, an economic awareness, an experience of politics, a sense of the individual in society, a feeling for other people in other places, a development of language, an enjoyment of reading, watching, listening, writing, drawing, acting...

I have heard it said — and I understand the point — that the term 'integrated' oughtn't to be used: it implies a series of pre-existing categories which are to be brought together and might be cobbled together. That is certainly one way of seeing it. But the argument of the contributions which follow point to a special meaning for the term 'integrated', a meaning which is interchangeable with 'integral'. If all the areas of understanding, feeling and experience enumerated above are seen to be of the essence of an integrated approach — and the list is left deliberately incomplete — then we are involved in something very different from conventional practice, and the difference does not reside in the lack of subject divisions or labels. From necessity, in fact, a curricular revolution is being born. What, essentially, integrated humanities implies is that learning about *human affairs* is learning about *human beings.* It has taken an economic ice-age to make us realize that the learning activity involved is fundamentally different from that involved in learning about the axiomatic logic of maths or the material nature of physical substance or the nervous coordination of our muscles. Of course, logic and physical experience and coordination are certainly going to be involved — but they will not be the defining characteristics of this 'humanistic' learning. The learning experience in humanities is not really to do with 'study', in its usual sense at all: nor, on the other hand, is it simply about 'activity'. It is about a process which is best described I suppose as, precisely, 'experience'. When someone (and not only someone young) 'learns' something in a real sense about human existence, that person is *experiencing* a link between the self and the conditions of life of the species. This does not happen by simply seeing it written down, still less by being told about it: it happens, precisely, 'by experience' that is, by an act of personal involvement. Now Jerome Bruner and others have argued, powerfully, for this as a defining characteristic of *all* true learning. What is being said, in that case, is that information about the physical universe or a proposition in maths can be converted into humanistic learning — not surprisingly, since the physical universe is *the* condition of human existence and propositional constructs are an age-old human strategy for coping with it. I am far from wanting to deny a humanism to science and maths education — and our continued existence as a species will depend on our recognizing technology as being *by* humans *for* humans. But in the reality of schools we have to draw the line somewhere — at least temporarily. Let's first get our house in order in that area of the curriculum that we choose to think of as 'the humanities'. Some of the contributors to this volume are already reaching out towards a 'whole school' philosophy, but they do so diffidently, not wanting to appear imperialistic.

The argument here is that the general area of humanities requires — or ought to require — a method of learning which is 'involving'.

3

Whereas people have learned a great deal about technology or about the properties of matter without necessarily feeling a great deal of 'involvement' with the physical objects of their endeavour, no one has ever really learned about themselves in relation to others ('humanistic' learning) without such involvement. So if Bruner, for instance, urges the experiential approach to maths or chemistry he is really urging an approach which emphasizes the human significance of these areas of knowledge. He wants the school to encourage 'young mathematicians' and 'young scientists' in the sense that they re-enact the experience of really *being* mathematicians and scientists, that is, being people who are breaking new ground in those areas. Fine. We certainly need to 'humanize' and demystify such things — especially for those who are least likely to ever *be* scientists or mathematicians. But what is being argued in relation to integrating 'the humanities' is that this sort of learning is not fundamentally about observation, measurement, hypothesis-making or even 'study' — though all these things may well be involved. The skills which we wish to develop for everyone in humanities as part of a 'core' area of learning are skills of a different order from those we are told schools should be developing on an optional basis for specific individuals — operating a capstan lathe or a word processor, for instance. They are even different from those which we may wish individuals to develop within the traditional areas of the conventional 'humanities' faculty — the skill of cartography, perhaps, as opposed to the ability to understand the way cartographers turn three dimensions into two. For the confusing thing about secondary schools is that the same people — both teachers and learners — are involved with these two very different sorts of skills at different moments on the timetable. Sometimes they are developing specific prevocational skills, at others they are developing general 'human' ones. Until quite recently the dominant model for the secondary school, in fact, was prevocational — whether the 'vocation' was professional or technical. As comprehensive education matures, the dominant model is becoming 'developmental' and the prevocational activity is being restricted to its appropriate — and optional — sphere. This has inevitably led to a certain nervousness on the part of professional politicians of all parties: after all, if schools are involved more and more in what is actually 'political' in a fundamental sense, important consequences may follow for the practice of politics in a narrower sense. So the cry is raised that schools should be preparing young people for the 'real' world of work and a pressure builds up for a truly Victorian valuation of education as vocational preparation.

But the proper response to such narrowness does not consist in vainly defending the *status quo*. What the contributions to this collection offer, in proposing integrated humanities as a central activity for the school, is an alternative version of 'preparing the young for the real world'. This version doesn't pretend that what we do in schools can directly affect the economy; it denies credibility to the rain-dance invocations of politicians. The ills of the economy are real and they won't go away, but they weren't created in the first place by some missing ingredient in the education of a potential work force and they shouldn't be visited upon teachers and students. Nevertheless the sort of curriculum described here *is* concerned with economics as an important part of understanding how each individual fits into a world picture. It *is* concerned to discover the operations of the world market, the implications of 'high tech', the point of decision which lies behind the development of a scientific discovery, the interests which promote research into this rather than that aspect of the physical universe. Always a humanities curriculum will accustom the learner in school to look for the human motivation and the self-interest in things commonly portrayed as 'mechanisms' somehow above and beyond human decision or determination. It will seek always to promote the understanding of events in our world in terms of the human actors in them. For, as time goes on, most of these events *are* the result of human intervention — the weather not excluded. We now know that we should not understand drought in Africa as a visitation from God, still less the result of blind fate. Neither should we see the misery of the 'Third World' in general as unrelated to our conditions of life in the 'First World'. A study of interdependence is an important element in any integrated humanities programme.

But simply to 'study' something does not of itself lead to the sort of comprehension which a good humanities teacher aims at: you can 'understand' things without 'comprehending' them in the way implied by humanistic learning. An active comprehension requires that the springs of human *feeling* be tapped. It requires, certainly, a simple understanding that, to however minor a degree, we are all responsible for what happens in the world, but it also involves a *moral feeling* about that responsibility. Such a level of comprehension is certainly not widespread in Britain at the moment. The bleak economic climate tends to produce, on the contrary, a sort of 'social psychopathology' — a deficiency in moral feeling and sense of shared responsibility. The ills of the world tend, rather, to be blamed on the victims. Pity is in short supply. In such a context humanities learning in schools becomes more than ever important, especially that part of it which aims to develop the skill of empathy. For without a sense of shared feeling no amount of *information* will be of avail; if the learners simply 'switch off' when the topic is too demanding on their emotions they will never learn in a humanistic way, never comprehend.

Humanities teachers frequently need to approach the most important issues tangentially therefore. Several of the contributors refer to the importance of narrative. It is seen in the use of good documentary video material which appeals to the 'human interest' in what is being portrayed and has a strong sense of journalistic story-line. Here, as elsewhere, humanities teachers have learnt from the practice of journalists — people who have to *sell* their topic in terms of narrative, of story. This approach, used carefully, can lead to interest and sympathy. Empathy takes longer.

Those — and I am one — who argue that *English* ought to be involved in any real humanities integration do so partially because English is the traditional curricular vehicle for story — not least the learner's story. By the process of imaginative projection, in writing or drama, the humanities learner can move towards a genuine sharing of feeling, an empathy. A British adolescent who has recently viewed, say, a video about someone of the same age in Brazil, may be readier to turn to a story about contemporary life in Latin America, will begin to take more notice of factual material about monoculture or the *latifundia* system, will look more carefully at photographs of a *favella*; having read further material, say, in biographical form — she or he will be ready to act out the experience of a destitute peasant newly arrived in the city. Having more deeply 'comprehended' the data, such a learner will be better prepared to undertake the cognitive task of making links between her/himself and the denizen of the *favella*. This, I suspect, is the way round that is most likely to induce real learning of a 'factual' sort. It is also the background for developing the whole range of analytic skills which lead to a growth in intelligent participation in the world. But such analytical activity is, for most people, a slow and painful process — a point often missed by teachers, precisely because they are of the minority who have usually found it relatively easy and enjoyable. For most people this sort of intellectualization needs to be constantly reinforced by imaginative projection: by reading, writing and enacting and — quite simply, by *enjoyment*.

But the centrality of these aspects of English to the experience of learning in the humanities is not only a matter of enabling imaginitive connections to be made in relation to specific issues. Good English teaching has, as a goal, the personal enlargement of the learner through vicarious but powerful experience — not least in the heightened area of the poetic, whether in metric or prose form. It is important that people are enabled, in the only setting in modern life where this is likely, to express their thoughts and feelings in their own 'language' — both verbally and, through enactment, in an extra-verbal way. In my own teaching experience I was often astounded by the ability of *very* 'non-academic' young people to use highly-controlled movement to express — usually — humour. This 'clowning' tradition is one that is widely understood even in our bureaucratized society — and one too seldom explored by teachers. It has very little to do with understanding the specific content of humanities lessons, of course. Most often it is employed against the teacher, as an expression of defiance. But, given its proper place in the curriculum as a part of drama, it has a more fundamental use: it builds, curiously, the self-respect of the 'clown'. And it is on self-respect that humanities learning depends.

This is true more generally. Even the least exhibitionist person has strengths and interests — often in decorative directions. Anyone who thinks the ornate cover to a folder of coursework is not part of the work has missed something essential about how people come to terms with social existence — including that part of it spent in learning. The 'self-concept', as the psychologists say, of the learner is the living foundation on which the skilled humanities teacher builds. And it is for this sort of reason, as much as for what they can do to build bridges to the unfamiliar, that the 'creative' subjects of English, drama and design are such a necessary ingredient of humanities in an integral sense.

Much of what is being argued here will be familiar to those engaged in primary education — though if the various surveys of primary *practice* are to be believed, it has a certain flavour of rarity about it there also. I often wonder whether this is because much good intent is enjoined 'from above' in primary education rather than arising from the expediency of the teachers — headteachers always excepted, of course! If so this has much to do with the 'self-image' of the primary teacher herself (statistically it is most likely to be *her*self). The difference in the experience of the women and men who have contributed to this volume — and among good humanities practitioners it was not difficult to achieve a gender-balance — is that, as secondary teachers, they enjoy a relative autonomy. They are also often 'academically well qualified' — meaning that their qualifications carry a fairly high social valuation — which helps them at a school level to employ pragmatism more easily. Having said this, though, all of the contributors to this collection would certainly acknowledge an indebtedness to the visible achievements of so many primary teachers in the very approaches secondary teachers of humanities most need to develop. Those who teach the younger secondary range are obviously most closely involved in consciously extending good practice from primary to secondary schools, and integrated humanities provides an ideal vehicle with which to achieve this extension. But it is not a question of 'transition', implying that less formal and hidebound methods in the early secondary years are no more than a preparation for increased narrowness and conventionalism in the older classes. The experience reported in what follows has often been quite the reverse — the needs of the older 'student' (surely the most appropriate term for adolescent learners?) are what has dictated the employment of more active and involved learning in the humanities. Throughout the country it is now more typically the fourth and fifth years which are being introduced to integrated approaches stressing process and skills — a situation which has both encouraged and been stimulated by the development of new GCSE syllabi entitled 'Integrated Humanities'. This has resulted in what I might term the 'sandwich effect' — integrated approaches in year one and sometimes year two, traditional approaches in year three and integrated approaches again in years four and five.

Pragmatism is certainly involved here, given the problem of staffing separate humanities subjects at the 16+ exam level. Pragmatism is also involved in the use of TVEI programmes to pump-prime and popularize integrated approaches from 14 to 16, and pragmatism is about to be employed again in current plans to develop the new Certificate of Prevocational Education (CPVE) at the post-16 level — a syllabus which specifically encourages a process and skills-based approach involving an integrated core of general education. But it is an enlightened and principled pragmatism — part of a creative response to adversity which is producing the developments described in this volume.

What the teachers who have contributed the following chapters share in common — they are otherwise quite diverse in age, subject-background and previous experience — is a sort of creative practicality. While none of them is afraid of theory, each of them in her or his own way is a successful and admired classroom practitioner. Like many of those others who are to be found involved in integrated humanities from Deeside to Wearside and from Yorkshire down to the south coast, they do not see practical survival as a problem distinct from theoretical advance. In a time of widespread demoralization in the profession they try, against all odds, to combine being good 'teacher activists', solid in their support of necessary sanctions, with a determination to maintain and improve the learning of their students. As the economy declines, as youth unemployment worsens, as education cuts are compounded by cuts in other public services, the *education* of the next generation, the improvement of its level of intelligence, sensitivity and world-mindedness becomes ever more vital. 'Humanities in a cold climate' maybe, but humane none the less. We must never lose hold of *that*.

Why Integrate?

John Haslam

It is unfortunate that, at present, a move towards integration within the humanities in some secondary schools is one step in an essentially defensive strategy to preserve the more traditional areas of the curriculum against the demands for extended space by the more directly vocational subjects. The influence of the MSC through its TVEI scheme is forcing schools to search for ways in which they can give greater prominence to those courses which are thought to provide the skills that can be easily and quickly transferred to work environments. Any new courses that might be added to the curriculum these days will almost certainly have their accent on vocationalism: business studies, CDT, information technology, engineering science — these are the subjects that schools are looking to expand at the moment, and, if it is possible for them to add options to the package that they offer their third year students, it will almost certainly be from within these areas. I say 'if it is possible' because declining school rolls are making it very difficult indeed for schools to add to their range of subjects. In the 1970s new courses could be bolted on to the curriculum package of a school without too much difficulty: a new specialist teacher could be brought in; increasing student numbers meant that the viability of other subjects would not be threatened by the addition of further courses; schools could tolerate luxurious staff/student ratios in minority subjects. In such an atmosphere teachers were encouraged to develop new 'mode three' exam syllabuses and to extend the range of options available to fourth year students. New academic interests that were making an impact in higher education could be translated into syllabuses that were appropriate to the 16-year-old, no matter what their direct vocational relevance might be. New areas of knowledge and new approaches within more traditional subjects could be added to the curriculum as courses in their own right, without the reservations that the school could not afford them in terms of staffing, time and space, which are the prevailing concerns of deputy heads involved in timetabling in the 1980s.

Thus it is clear that the humanities are in a particularly vulnerable position at the present time. The new vocationalism pressurizes schools to direct their curriculum thinking to TVEI type courses; this is where the money will be spent and where the new staff will be recruited: when the historian exits, on walks the information technologist. 'History is a thing of the past' sums up the cynicism in the Humanities Faculty at my own school. At the same time, declining rolls make it difficult for schools to make any additions to their provision, and therefore new courses are almost always installed at the expense of old ones. There is therefore a double squeeze on the humanities. The further rub is that this is taking place at a time when humanities teachers are coming under attack nationally because of the politically sensitive areas which form the subject-matter of many of their courses. It is not surprising that defensiveness reaches the brink of paranoia when these threats are borne in mind.

A common response by schools is to consolidate the *core curriculum*. Conceding the options to the new vocationalism, they have given up the idea of maintaining a wide range of humanities specialisms on the market stall of the third year option sheet. Instead they have argued for the establishment of humanities within the compulsory area of the curriculum (in the fourth and fifth years) with a view to concentrating their resources either within a small range of subjects, or in a common course which utilizes an integrated approach. It is in the discussion about which of these two alternatives should be adopted that the divisions among the humanities staff begin to appear. The teachers of the more traditional 'high status' subjects such as history and geography usually argue that choice should be maintained, and prefer to guard their subject identities within the core curriculum. Their argument is that every student should study a humanities subject up to the age of 16, and the full range that the school can offer should be available to them within the core curriculum. The problem here for the administrators is that this arrangement does not alleviate the 'inefficiencies' in staffing and the 'clutter' of the curriculum which is frowned on so much these days. Their tendency is to 'rationalize' the subjects — to eliminate overlap, and as far as possible keep the choice narrow so that classes can be staffed efficiently and resources can be deployed economically. In these circumstances it tends to be history, geography and social studies which retain (or gain) their place within the core, after the 'weeding out' of environmental studies, economics, sociology and others. The prospect of this outcome can provoke an alliance between the administrators and the minority specialists around the proposal to institute an integrated course which utilizes the methods and perspectives of the different humanities disciplines, and thus preserves the primary (i.e., core) objective of ensuring that all students come into contact with the distinctive learning experiences that the humanities provide. For the administrators this solution conveniently renders humanities as efficient to timetable as English and maths. For the teachers of the humanities minority subjects it is a vehicle for retaining part of their subject, and it prevents history and geography escaping unpruned from the administrators' secateurs.

It is possible, therefore, to arrive at integrated humanities (henceforth 'IH') via this very negative route. Integration is part of a purely defensive strategy — administratively convenient, efficiently utilizing potentially redundant staff while making it unnecessary to replace others in order to preserve a specific discipline, and permitting schools to divert their declining resources to prevocational areas of education which will, we are assured, 'build a better Britain'. This is a very different scenario from the early 1970s when IH was consciously and willingly established in the core curriculum for very positive and constructive reasons. It was not then a strategy for the defence of a rump humanities, but a vehicle for a more ·realistic and rewarding method than any one of the particular disciplines could afford of developing skills, and learning about salient contemporary issues. It is worth rehearsing the positive arguments for integration that were outlined in that period of educational change, at a time when it might appear as though integration is the last bunker for a humanities staff fighting back the combined forces of the MSC, declining rolls, and Roger Scruton.

When we justify the place of IH within the school curriculum it is important to register that the justification is for a component of the *core* curriculum. The reasoning for this is of the same order of argumentation by which the essential subjects of maths and English are secured within the core. It is therefore very different from saying that 'every student should study at least one humanities subject but it does not really matter which'. If humanities is to be part of the compulsory core curriculum for every student, then it must be not a separate discipline, but *integrated* humanities. Schools will have done a disservice to 16-year-olds who have not by that age investigated in some formal way the major issues that affect human beings in the world today, and which provide the main menu for most daily news bulletins on television and in print. That is certainly part of the justification for the place of the content IH within the core curriculum. It is the responsibility of the Humanities Department to furnish some perspectives and background knowledge to students on the kinds of contemporary issues which form the subject matter of social conversation about the world, whether that conversation takes place in the public house, the tennis club, or the *Newsnight* studio. It is also the responsibility of humanities to develop in students the skills that will enable them to handle information about those issues. There are two arguments which can be marshalled to demonstate why IH, rather than any one separate discipline, is better able to fulfil these educational objectives. One concerns the *factual content* which we would want the students to tackle, and the other covers the nature of the *skills* that we would want the students to develop.

The kinds of issues and problems that have achieved prominence in the modern world which would form the themes or topics of an IH course cannot be categorized under the labels of traditional disciplines. To be studied in a rounded and realistic way they require an investigation which utilizes perspectives and knowledge that cross subject boundaries. Is it possible, for example, to study any trouble spot in the contemporary world without reference to both sociological and geographical perspectives? And can the famines of Eastern Africa be comprehended without looking closely at the economic, environmental, and political backgrounds? If humanities is to be a part of the compulsory curriculum then salient issues such as these should form the content of the course, and, if this is accepted, that content can only be studied realistically through an integrated approach that is free to draw upon the resources of *any* subject discipline in order to facilitate a full understanding of each issue.

Secondly, the skills that core humanities should develop are those that will in general terms help students to make sense of information about the world in both their working and social milieu. These are the skills of location and selection, interpretation and evaluation, and communication of information in various forms. All humanities subjects incorporate these skills within their separate syllabus objectives, but in each discipline they are tied to subject-specific concepts which render them academic and less transferable to real life. IH prioritizes the intellectual value that these skills undoubtedly hold and which is at the heart of all the separate humanities disciplines, without constraining the flexibility of those skills by hooking them to subject-specific concepts, many of which can be unnecessarily esoteric. It is the various topics of study which will determine the particular conceptual tools that are to be utilized in their investigation. This may well involve calling upon a particular discipline to make available a concept that is a traditional item in its own intellectual baggage, but the aim is to understand the *topic*, not the *discipline*, therefore the concept is only useful in so far as it assists in that understanding. IH encourages active investigation of varied and changing topics which provide the material on which these general order skills can be applied. But IH is not a fixed body of knowledge; nor is it a discipline defined by a limited set of concepts and methodologies. It is because it is not either of these that it can claim to have a place in the core curriculum.

Returning to the argument about the defensiveness felt by the traditional humanities subjects, it is interesting to note the way in which several of the new GCSE subject criteria in the humanities seek to emphasize the possible complementary perspectives that should be incorporated within each syllabus. It is as if each one independently were laying claim to be the subject which can stand as the true focus for integration — the central hub for the other subject spokes. It would seem that each is vaguely recognizing that it deals with subject matter that it cannot justify laying sole claim to; each syllabus recognizes that there are other humanities perspectives which can legitimately inform the field of knowledge which has been traditionally its prerogative. Reluctantly accepting the implications of this recognition, and belatedly realizing that the curricular wolves are at the door, each one puts in its bid to be the humanities discipline which is at the essential heart of this area of the curriculum. In each case the justification seeks to show how other perspectives can be incorporated within the specific discipline in order to provide a more thorough, rounded, balanced understanding of the subject's content. Since each syllabus separately is making the same noises, it is not too difficult to see that putting them all in the same band would merely require the orchestration of integrated humanities to get a decent tune out of them.

Sir Keith Joseph's speech to the Geographical Association as reported in the *Times Educational Supplement* of 21 June 1985 illustrates a similar angle on this situation. His speech is crowded with comments about the complex relationships that make up the world, the study of which

> ought to help pupils come to understand the intricate economic, social and political interconnections between different parts of the world and between factors which determine what happens in any particular part of it.

He is addressing geographers, but he is talking about integrated humanities. He acknowledges that

> the skills of history and geography, though different, have much in common, for example in the weighing of evidence which is

complex, incomplete, conflicting, and itself influenced by sub-
jective factors.

Why restrict such skills to just history and geography? They are the
skills that underpin the method of *all* humanities subjects. In fact, Sir
Keith's speech to the geographers overflows with assertions and reasoning which could be unproblematically ascribed to a powerful justification for IH. A remarkable intervention; and one which was no doubt
welcomed by those geographers who recognize that geography must
cover a wider canvas if it is to remain viable within the core curriculum,
but which was possibly greeted with incredulity by the more
traditionally-minded geographers who saw their carefully defined
academic discipline reeling under the weight of the varied impedimenta
it was being asked to take on board.

What are the educational benefits of integrated humanities to the
students and the teachers? First of all an IH course will encourage
relevance, flexibility and choice in content. It is up to the staff to draw
up their syllabus. They decide on the topics, the study of which will
provide the students with the most appropriate background for assessing their personal relationship to the local, national and global issues of
the forseeable future. This encourages teamwork and the sharing of
ideas and information in the preparation of materials. As the resources
for the course are extended and varied it becomes more feasible to allow
the students themselves greater autonomy in choosing the content of
their study and the methods they wish to employ.

An IH course should encourage experiential learning of various
kinds. Self-directed enquiry into issues and topics is a key objective of
the approach, and this will, if the appropriate guidance is given,
stimulate students to pursue lines of investigation independently and
with increasing self-motivation. The onus is on the teachers to provide
students not with processed textbook-type material, but with primary
sources collected by the team (perhaps with the assistance of students)
and presented to students in a neutral way, requiring them to do the
processing, in order to use these sources in the presentation of accounts
and arguments through a variety of media. An IH course is an excellent
vehicle for group work, independent study, negotiated learning, problem solving, and other learning methods which have achieved interest
and support within education during the past decade.

Many of these approaches are of course not unique to IH; but the
wide compass of the approach serves to facilitate them. However, it
could be argued that some single humanities subjects and some
curriculum initiatives in other areas, have made greater progress in

promoting more productive learning techniques of a similar nature to the ones mentioned above, largely because they have had the status to attract a high level of national finance which has been used to fund experimental projects that have since become well-established curriculum innovations. The Schools Council projects in history and geography have developed an impressive range of materials which foster the skills of interpretation and evaluation of evidence. The new CPVE course promotes the practice of a negotiated and semi-independent programme of study which also relies on an integrated approach. Tutorial programmes in some schools have been used as the framework for tackling various social and moral issues which could also readily form the topics of an IH course.

Because of its historically marginalized status within the national educational consciousness, IH has found itself left behind in comparison with the publicity surrounding some other initiatives and the impact they have had on schools. Just as we were astonished to notice the separate humanities disciplines appropriating the ideology of integration in order to support their continuation as key subjects at GCSE, it is ironic to witness a prevocational course like CPVE adopting teaching styles and learning methods that are pure integrated humanities. Curriculum initiatives in other areas have made use of national networks to coordinate and consolidate innovation. Until recently IH has had no equivalent network to facilitate a sharing of ideas and resource production. Teachers were isolated in their schools, often expending energies duplicating the same strategies that were being developed in the school down the road, or at least in the next county. The point being made here is that, unless its supporters quickly regain some lost ground, the rationale for integration, and the methods of learning that are concomitant with it, will be surreptitiously detached from integrated humanities where they began, only to be contradictorarily inserted within the political justifications for any one of the single subjects, or, without due acknowledgement, associated with new courses that in other respects are little to do with the educational import of integrated humanities.

From what has been said so far it will come as no surprise that there will be considerable opposition from many specialist subject teachers towards any plan to introduce IH as the core humanities course within a school's curriculum. Such opposition is often fundamentally territorial: an unwillingness to see the demise of a subject, whatever the educational arguments for an alternative. I regard such a position as educationally untenable, since it is protecting a professional niche within an institution rather than justifying an area of education beneficial to students. This is perfectly understandable, but it is not an argument which should be allowed to win the educational day. However, there are objections of an *educational* nature to the abandonment of single subjects in favour of an integrated course, and these must be answered.

First of all there is the objection that teachers are specialists, and, having been trained to teach a particular subject, are unqualified to teach in other areas. There is a concern that teachers who feel insecure with the subject matter and method will teach badly — confused in the preparation of their lessons, hesitating in the explanation of the themes, vague in their expectations of the students. Referring specifically to the *factual content* of what is taught, this situation is no different from the subject department which decides to teach a new syllabus for the first time. For the historian who has been accustomed to teaching social and economic British history, a switch to twentieth century world history or Schools Council history is like taking on a completely new subject. A vast amount of material has to be assimilated before the teacher can feel confident and comfortable with the subject-matter of the new course. For the sociologist who has been familiar with domestic themes in syllabuses, the decision to introduce a topic such as under-development involves a major commitment to researching and mastering new material for which no previous experience can provide any easy short-cut. The first answer, therefore, is to point out that the challenge of taking on new subject material of a very different nature is not a problem which is specific to the setting up of an IH course; it is one which faces all departments whose subjects cover a wide content area. It might be objected to this that within single subjects there is usually a textbook which can provide a backbone of essential content, around which the teachers can build a more detailed and sophisticated body of knowledge. Although a textbook gives security to both the students and the teachers, it has many disadvantages even within single subject specialisms. The textbook is often the crutch which the teacher never abandons; it becomes the central focus of learning, rendering other approaches peripheral. A course then becomes a weekly march through the chapters of a textbook. This is a caricature of the worst kind of teaching, but it remains a constant danger whenever the textbook is the central resource. Even in those approaches which prioritize skills and conceptual understandings such as the Schools Council History Project, the availability of textbooks for several sections of the course detracts from the laudable objectives which are the Project's raison d'etre. Thus 'medicine through time', for example, becomes a twenty week race through the detail of three textbooks, in the hands of teachers who approach this section chronologically. Hence the attempt by the Avon Resources Development Unit to provide materials which assist the construction of a more thematic method of teaching the basic concepts of continuity and change and the ideas related to them.

The decision to adopt a new syllabus or devise a new course is rarely taken by just one teacher. If IH is introduced as the core humanities course to which all subject specialists will contribute, then it will probably involve the expertise and energies of quite a large group of teachers. There are several advantages to this which will help calm the fears of those who are concerned about the insecurity of teaching about topics they feel are divorced from their traditional subject-matter. The course outline must be planned as a team, and the issues and topics chosen must be agreed, probably unanimously. The investigation of each topic appropriate to an IH course will inevitably demand the utilization of perspectives, concepts and knowledge from a number of specialisms. Therefore the team as a whole will have an essential role to play in the preparatory thinking-through of the ways in which the topic can be studied and the kinds of work that the students will be expected to tackle. This initial process will begin to erase worries about the relevance of some specialisms, because it will quickly become apparent that all subjects have a contribution to make to the study of almost any topic, and that there are many connections implicit already in the way that single subjects have investigated related topics within the isolation of their separate departments in the past. It will also become clear that when a broad topic becomes the primary focus for the more didactic elements of the teaching, rather than the detailed concepts of a discipline, then the command of knowledge required will not be conceptually intricate. ('Interest' in the topic is a different question and will be dealt with later.)

So early planning will allay some insecurities. An important benefit of IH as a core course is then the opportunity to divide up the detailed preparation of material for the chosen topics of the course among quite a large team of teachers. It is possible to set up small working groups, each with the responsibility of collecting resources, preparing teaching materials, and working out the teaching details of different approaches, who will then report back to the whole team. This means that any one teacher is unlikely to be involved in the detailed preparation of more than one fourth and one fifth year topic, and will be able to rely on others to look after the resourcing of other areas of the course. Thus preparation does not become the unbearable load that is typical of the small department of three or four teachers who face the task of setting up an equivalent two-year course with just as many separate and different elements within it. The workload pressures of starting a new course do not depend on student numbers, but on the number of different sections to the course and the number of teachers who can share the work of preparation. IH as a core course makes resource-based learning instigated and researched by the teachers a realistic and acceptable objective in terms of preparation workload because of the comparatively large team involved. There is also the advantage that the task of explaining the materials and approaches to other teachers is a way of testing them before putting them into effect in the classroom; if they do not make sense to the teachers, then they are not likely to make sense to the students. There is immediate feedback and the opportunity to add and develop further ideas for each topic. Through these discussions the initial worries about competence and expertise can be overcome, as it becomes clear that the ways into the content are numerous and require the varied strengths of different subject teachers. It is possible for teachers to share ideas and teach each other — a situation which often produces pedagogic outcomes that are more than the sum of the parts. And when it comes to the classroom situation, it is a feasible and beneficial technique to employ different specialists when giving the lead lessons on the different topics of the course.

Connected with the 'lack of competence' objection, but less relevant, is the assertion that a teacher loves her/his subject and so do her/his students; therefore, why should s/he divert energies into a course which s/he will not really enjoy teaching and which is unlikely to offer her/him the context in which to generate enthusiasm in students for the particular subject? This is a perfectly valid point of view when looking at optional subjects. But when justifying a core element of the curriculum which the school is imposing on students, then teachers should prioritize the arguments that show the importance of the content and skills in terms of their educational value to the students. At this level the educationalist will recognize the relevance and applicability of the kind of work that is done within IH, as opposed to the narrower, more academic concern with learning a discipline that the specialist subject offers.

On the issue of enjoyment, it is probably true that all students will enjoy any subject that is 'taught well'. IH has the advantage that it facilitates the teaching of topics which generally resonate with the concerns and interests of students in their lives outside school, and it also encourages a strong element of student choice over a wide area of subject matter. These flexibilities carry with them the danger of unstructured fluidity which students are likely to reject, but then that would be the result of bad planning, just as would the negative responses shown by students towards a course that is too tightly prescriptive in its demands.

It is perhaps a luxury in the present climate for a teacher to expect to teach one single subject and nothing else. Schools demand a greater flexibility from their staff these days; this is an organizational point. But intellectually too, and at higher academic levels, the boundaries between disciplines have been, and are still, breaking down. It would be narrow-minded and anti-educational not to reflect this in the reorientations of the curriculum at secondary level. In both intellectual and administrative terms we can no longer afford the subject specialist whose own academic preferences blinker him/her to the confines of an extremely restricted field of study in the belief that this will guarantee both the enlightenment of mankind in general and the reproduction of the race of specialists, of which s/he is a member.

However, IH should not be the means whereby we are all turned into social studies teachers, which a wary subject specialist might well argue was the likely result of a thematic approach to the humanities. IH should not be watered-down sociology. Nor should it be social studies in the 'body of knowledge' sense. It is up to the core team to ensure that in the exploration of contemporary issues, the varied perspectives that each subject can make available are actually used in the most productive way possible to stimulate understanding, and the desire of students to find out more, independently. If such variety is not introduced, then the course *is* likely to collapse into a rather weak (i.e., broad) form of social studies.

A further 'academic' concern of the specialist teacher is that there will not be anything for the students to 'get their teeth into'. It is feared that the course will be too eclectic, and the students will drift through a rather unstructured haphazard collection of topics, unable to form a whole picture of what it is that they have been studying. It should be clear immediately that this objection rests on the false assumption that IH is a 'subject'. If anything is to give an IH course some sense of identity it will be the learning techniques that students are required to adopt. The level of generality of the information-handling skills that the course promotes probably will not give the students a sense of unity. The topic content will not necessarily appear as an obvious entity in the students' eyes either. The distinctiveness of IH for the students is most likely to result, rather, from the experiences they have during the investigation of the material. Such experiences will be an amalgamation of group discussion, individual enquiry, and mixed presentation (individual and group) of information relevant to any particular issue, and this will be the pattern for assessed work throughout the course. It is especially through the continual reinforcement of the idea that the students *themselves* can add by independent enquiry to the body of knowledge about a topic that students will recognize a central element of the course and therefore its individuality. As for 'getting their teeth' into things, this really depends on the quality of the teaching and the availability of accessible information about the topics studied. This is a question of how coursework assignments are approached and the kind of work that the students are expected to produce. Such questions are discussed elsewhere in the volume, but it is worth remembering here that a key objective of IH is to view issues carefully from all angles, and therefore superficiality should not be a fault of such a course.

Another worry of the subject specialist is that students involved in IH will be ill-prepared to take up 'A' level work in the separate subjects. One answer to this is to point out that some subjects do not at the moment insist that a student has studied the subject at fourth and fifth year level before taking up the subject in the sixth-form. So why should some subjects claim this advantage as a necessity, if, indeed, it is an advantage? Looking at the question more positively, IH may in fact be a better preparation for 'A' level work in all humanities subjects because of its questioning approach to issues, its concentration on interpretative and enquiry skills, and its emphasis on the open status of knowledge. This is not to say that single humanities could not and do not sometimes show these qualities, but that, in refusing to set itself up as a distinct body of knowledge, IH is more able to develop skills which have general applicability across a range of courses at sixth-form level.

I acknowledged earlier that changes within the teaching of some single subjects had brought about impressive developments in the 'skills' approach to learning. Some teachers might say that the work done for the history and geography Schools Council projects has produced techniques and materials which are now sufficiently well-established to influence all teachers to adopt a more skills-based approach to teaching all humanities subjects, and that the quality of their materials has led students to produce work of greater insight and analytical sophistication than could ever be achieved through some rather vague generalized investigation of contemporary issues. The achievements of the Schools Council were undeniably impressive. But, significantly, it no longer exists. In the future teachers are likely to receive and generate more support by collaborative work within their own schools on courses that a large team can contribute to, while applying, with due acknowledgement, many of the techniques that the Schools Council pioneered. Secondly, the history and geography projects, although they develop critical perspectives, still focus the students' attentions on subject matter that is of itself esoteric and of little intrinsic interest to the majority of 16-year-olds. This is not to say that teachers cannot successfully generate interest in material that is considerably distanced from students' experience; nor is it to deny the place of these subjects in the curriculum. Given that time is short, though, any core humanities course should be helping students to develop an awareness of the context of issues which are important in the world today, which means, for example, looking at super-power rivalry and its origins, rather than, say, the motivations behind Elizabethan diplomacy.

Justifications for IH at the level of educational theory are necessary, but on their own they will not convince teachers — particularly those who in recent years have put enormous effort and thought into establishing new courses within their own subjects which go a long way towards developing the style of teaching that is associated with IH. This effort and the undoubtedly impressive work that has come out of it, account for the strength of feeling that lies behind the arguments of those who resist IH on the lines of the last objection to it described above. IH will only convince the most hardened sceptics of its worth by the results of its practice. It is not possible to show these (i.e., students' work) in a book of this sort, but a more detailed description of the activities and methods that are associated with IH courses can be given, and this is what several of the other contributions are concerned with.

The Role of Language Support

Viv Styles

Being socio-economically disadvantaged is no simple matter of deficit, of suffering a cultural avitaminosis that can be dosed by suitable inputs of compensation. It is a complex of circumstances at the centre of which is usually a family whose wage earner is without a job or where there is no male wage earner. If there is a job, usually it is as demeaning in status as it is unremunerative. The setting is a neighbourhood that has adapted itself often with much human bravura to 'being at the bottom', with little by way of long-range perspective or hope, often alienated by a sense of ethnic separation from the main culture.[1]

Moreton School is a community comprehensive in a designated social priority area of Wolverhampton. Many of its pupils suffer acute 'social deprivation' which is reflected in low attainment and under-achievement as well as poor motivation and low self-image. I began teaching at Moreton in 1980 when I worked in the Humanities Faculty. I struggled through my first year with a timetable of first and second year integrated humanities, fourth year history and fourth and fifth year social studies, all taught to mixed ability classes.

'Mixed ability' at Moreton means two to three children who can barely read and write, five or six who need a considerable amount of help, a further six to nine who would be considered low average and two or three more able pupils in each class of twenty-five or twenty-six. I began to realize how academically poor Moreton children are when I attended a DES course which focussed on 'average and less able pupils'. I discovered that everyone else's 'average' were my brighter pupils and their 'less able' were my average. The samples of work I took along were dismissed as the work of 'remedials' and therefore outside the realm of the ordinary class teacher. No one else had a child in her class who could not read.

When I first arrived in the Humanities Faculty at Moreton I was presented with armfuls of multi-coloured worksheets. There were blue worksheets for less-able pupils, white for average pupils and pink for the more-able. White and blue were watered down versions of the pink until concepts were stripped bare in an attempt to simplify language and content. In theory the children were all doing the same work and absorbing the same concepts. In practice the cries of 'Why is her worksheet blue?', 'Blue for thickies', and 'Why is mine different?' were drowning out the educational principles. The copying-out exercises for the 'blue pupils' taught them nothing and at best kept them quiet; at worst they were made into paper darts or just literally thrown out of the window.

By the time I had crawled out of my first year at Moreton I was beginning to understand the theories of language in learning which I had studied at college. The pupils were teaching me about 'talk in the classroom', and the pupils from whom I learned the most were the least able; those children who find it hard to concentrate for more than a couple of minutes; those children who happily engage in an entirely different task from the one I have spent ten minutes explaining; children who may indulge in aggressive or anti-social behaviour in an attempt to disguise their learning difficulties; children who find it hard to write half a dozen sentences, who find 'big words' hard to read and yet who have the ingenuity to build model igloos out of no resources, who will role play a seal hunt which is accurate in every detail and who will make up their own misspelt and ungrammatical but nevertheless entertaining creation stories or poems. The children taught me that they will not be divided into pink, white or blue, that they are individuals with their own experiences and interpretations and that instead of struggling to get them to listen to *me* I should be sitting back and listening to *them*.

I would like to take this opportunity to thank a child called John. John taught me how to understand precisely what Barnes, Britton *et al* meant by 'talk in the classroom'. The following dialogue is part of a transcript of a taped discussion by a group of second year pupils (aged 12) during a humanities lesson. The topic is old age. The children have been listening to a story about an old eskimo woman left out on the ice. The children are in friendship groups to discuss a number of questions relating to old age in *our* society. John's group was led by Mrs X the school's Curriculum Assistant. Her contributions are unobtrusive and encouraging. She does try to direct the group back to the questions but apart from a little gentle persuasion she lets the children do the talking. The contributions of the other children are just as important, but follow John's contribution.

Mrs X: Do you think they're lonely some of them?

Everyone: Yes.

Mrs X: Do you think that's one of the biggest things that bother them?

Brian: They don't usually have anybody to come and see them.

Justin: And they have pets.

Shaun: Dogs.

John: Cats.

Shaun: There's one next door to us and he's 85 and we have to keep watching him because in case he has a stroke or something . . .

Mrs X: Have your grandparents got pets?

John: My . . . my . . .

Justin: My nan's got twenty-two cats.

John: My . . . my . . .

Mrx X: How many?

Justin: Twenty-two.

John: My . . . my grandad . . .

Justin: And kittens.

John: . . . and my nan has got 400 fish in a big pool.

Shaun: They keep putting water in don't they?

Justin: They've got a dog as well.

Mrs X: They get very devoted to them don't they?

Shaun: A lot of old people do the gardening as well.

John: My grandad has a nice garden.

Justin: My grandad does the garden . . . and does he shout at you if you go on it?

John: No, he doesn't shout at us because there's a seat round the tree and you can sit on it and we just go round there.

Justin: If we step on his plants and that he shouts.

John: He shouts at us then . . . He's got some rockery and he's made some thingies you fill up with water and then it goes into the other one and then that one and then it goes into the pool.

Mrs X: Oh yes, like a waterfall . . . and has he got a pump or does he just fill the top one up and it all runs down?

John: And it all runs down.

Justin: And what's he made the pool from?

Shaun: Concrete . . . some plastic bags and polythene first . . .

John: Some . . . some . . . just a bit . . . the rockery bit was there. The pool was there but there was nothing in it. They took all the fish with them the last ones did . . . and our grandad had to do it up. It took him about two years.

Mrs X: So do you think your grandparents are happy then?
John: Sometimes they get angry when people run over the pool and chuck bricks in it . . .

John had not made any contributions to group discussion until this occasion. His written work was often incomprehensible and his reading slow and stilted. He often 'got stuck' on unfamiliar words. During class discussion the teacher would most certainly have directed talk away from John's grandad's fish pool towards more important and more relevant concepts relating to old age in society. In being given the opportunity to express his own experience in his own words, in the security of a small group of classmates, John was able to make an important step forward in terms of his own language development as well as personal development. From his first one word contribution, through his three stuttered attempts to join the discussion, to his long and complicated explanations John breaks through the language barrier so that even his rival Justin has to stop and listen and becomes interested enough to ask a question. He helps to turn a series of almost unrelated statements into the beginnings of conversation. John's friend Shaun offers valuable assistance but in the end it is not needed.

Here is an extract from a discussion by the same group of boys some weeks later. Mrs X is not present, the boys are on their own with a tape recorder. The topic is eskimo beliefs.

Brian: . . . and they believe that when they catch a fish they've got to put ashes on the eyes so the spirits of the soul don't warn its brothers and that, that they're going to be caught.
Justin: And what happens when one of them dies? Do they have . . . special things that they do to them?
Brian: We don't know do we?
Shaun: We never saw a film about that.
John: . . . and when they hunt the caribou they have to use . . . do . . . use like . . . What do they have to do?
Brian: They have to build *inukshuks* that look like men, of stones, and they drive the caribou down into the water.
John: Yes, yes and you know when there's thingy . . .
Shaun: With their kayaks.
John: . . . and you know when there's spirits . . .
Shaun: They spear them, with a spear.
John: Yes they spear them and then they cook them.
Brian: Yes, they cook them over a fire.
John: And the spirits don't like it if you cook them with grass on

25

the fire because they eat that and . . . they have to cook it over
something different.

Justin: . . . that the animal doesn't eat?

John: And the people, the eskimos catch it and they're kind to it
or else it won't get hunted again . . . the spirit.

Shaun: Yes, it just keeps going round.

John's progress is obvious. He not only joins the discussion but
makes an important contribution which displays a good conceptual grasp
of the topic. John and other like him convinced me of the value of
language in learning for all children but in particular for slow learners.

I have spent the last three years at Moreton working for the Special
Needs Department. As the language support coordinator I am responsible for organizing extra help for the less able pupils in years one to
three. I lead a team of twelve staff whose main teaching time is spent in
a variety of subject disciplines: modern languages, science, maths,
English, humanities and PE. The language support team helps slow
learners in one lesson a week of mixed ability humanities, one of science
and one of English. Each member of the team is attached to one or more
tutor groups and assumes some responsibility for the children who
experience learning difficulties. She will automatically form a sub-team
consisting of herself, the form tutor of her group and the subject staff
who teach her group. Upwards of fifty members of staff may be directly
involved in language support work. The number of pupils helped in
each class varies from four to eight. At present 110 pupils are receiving
language support in years one to three. The aims of the language
support team are as follows:

(a) To identify children experiencing learning difficulties in the full
class situation.

(b) To give individual attention to identified less able pupils.

(c) To develop a personal and meaningful dialogue with individuals
and to give them a secure framework within which to work.

(d) To encourage less able pupils to read and to see reading as an
enjoyable and meaningful activity.

(e) To encourage less able pupils to relate topics and content of
lessons to their own experience and to engage in meaningful
discussion.

(f) To monitor the progress of individuals.

(g) To work across the curriculum in the mixed ability situation.

(h) To enable slow learners to achieve success and develop confidence.

(i) To make contact with the parents of slow learners and invite their involvement and support.

(j) To work closely with subject teachers and form tutor to achieve the above aims and call a meeting of staff involved when appropriate to discuss the progress of identified slow learners.

The language support teacher is not a 'remedial' teacher and is not asked to be in the traditional sense of the term. The support teacher is not expected to be an expert in the teachng of literacy and need have no knowledge of reading schemes, reading ages, phonic rules or grammar skills. To quote Paulo Freire:

> Acquiring literacy does not involve memorizing sentences, words or syllables — lifeless objects unconnected to an existential universe — but rather an attitude of creation and re-creation, a self-transformation producing a stance of intervention in one's context.
>
> Thus the educator's role is fundamentally to enter into dialogue with the illiterate about concrete situations and simply to offer him the instruments with which he can teach himself to read and write.[2]

Any member of staff undertaking language support work is asked to adopt the philosophy of learning to read advocated by Frank Smith, Margaret Meek and others like B. Thompson:

> My philosophy is that you learn to read by reading. From this simple precept a number of things follow: that you learn to read better by reading more; that you learn to read really well by reading plenty of interesting, relevant material of high quality; and that motivation is more important than methodology.[3]

Children are encouraged to read as much and as widely as possible. They are given every opportunity to talk and write from their own experience. The support teacher works closely with subject staff to ensure that the children are given the chance to read books in lessons, to talk both in pairs and in small groups, to write expressively and imaginatively and to relate classwork to their own experience. With an extra teacher in the room to help with the 'difficult' pupils, subject staff feel more confident about tackling a groupwork lesson or bringing books into the classroom or turning an entire lesson over to free reading and discussion. In asking for these things for less able children the support team ensures that all children reap the benefits of this kind of approach.

The development of a whole-school policy on language in learning across the curriculum has meant that all departments are now examining their methods and resources for teaching mixed ability. Teachers are gaining the confidence to abandon worksheets in favour of books, and teacher talk in favour of pupil talk.

So what has become of the humanities pink, white and blue worksheets? They went out of the window a few years ago. Although I now teach English I am still an 'honorary member' of the Faculty and as a language support teacher to three classes a good proportion of my time is spent in the humanities area. Over the last term I have been involved in interviewing first and third year pupils about their humanities course. The list of suggested — but by no means compulsory — questions included 'What did you think about the topic on . . .?', 'What type of work do you like best . . .?' and 'Did you enjoy the topic on . . .?' as well as concept-based questions relating to the coursework. The interviewer is asked to assess the child's ability to communicate as well as her understanding of the concepts of the course of study. 'Less able' children are often the most successful pupils in this kind of assessment. The 'more able' children tend to regurgitate facts with little regard for the question or the relevance of their answers. 'Less able' pupils often grasp basic concepts almost without realizing it and are much better at relating their understanding to their own experience. Of course there are children who say very little and appear to understand even less. These children are often quiet, unassuming girls who lack the confidence to express an opinion, even in a small group.

It is becoming increasingly apparent that girls are disadvantaged in learning and that it is only through individual attention that some girls get the amount of support and encouragement they need. Even the least able boys are generally able to express themselves verbally and will often dominate both small group and class discussion. Some will talk constantly if only to disguise the fact that their writing is poor or their reading is less than fluent. Girls are more likely to settle down quickly to work, getting on quietly with their writing or reading to themselves. They are seldom found taking a dominant role in anything and consequently fail to develop their thinking and understanding, unless they can be encouraged to verbalize and redefine their experiences. During one humanities lesson I observed a second year group involved in fifteen minutes of class discussion. In spite of efforts to the contrary by the class teacher her attention was entirely taken up by the boys who were either shouting out or wildly waving their arms until they were noticed. Not one girl made a single contribution to the discussion. . . . The language support system enables those children who may be neglected in a whole class situation to receive the extra individual attention they need.

In addition to interviewing pupils, language support staff have been involved in role play, simulation games, craftwork and creative writing. I have taken the part of Passport Control Officer in a role play about immigration. I have assisted in the construction of a three-dimensional wall display of a model of the community undertaken by a first year group. I have helped a group of five second year pupils to devise a board game about survival in a developing country. I have taken part in a number of interesting and stimulating lessons from which I have gained as much as the children. Integrated humanities at Moreton consists of a first year course which has been developed from *Man: a Course of Study*: the Salmon, Herring Gull and Baboon units, a second year course developed from the MACOS Eskimo unit, and a third year course which — in a predominantly white working class area — looks at Britain as a multicultural society with work based on reasons for movement. Staff have taken the fundamental principles of MACOS and have used them to develop and extend the content to include units on a complex as well as simple society, world development, and the individual and the community. The third year course looks at immigration to Britain as well as emigration and involves studies of Asian, Aborigine, African and West Indian cultures as well as tackling prejudice and discrimination and challenging traditional historical perspectives.

As in any humanities course there is a wealth of opportunity for discussion on a vast range of topics. Humanities staff also actively encourage the reading of fiction and include stories, myths and legends in their study of a culture as well as presenting novels which are related to the unit content, for example, *Walkabout*. Language support staff are used as an extra resource to facilitate the kind of teaching methods which are considered relevant to all pupils. Children are encouraged to write their own newspapers, engage in creative work of all kinds from play writing to model making, use a wide range of audio-visual resources, undertake project/research work, design posters and information booklets for other pupils and to read whatever books are available. Assessment is in the form of profiles which comment on children's strengths and progress in language skills as well as acquisition and understanding of concepts. Humanities is an ideal environment in which to work with slow learners at Moreton.

The critics of language support complain because we do not teach grammar and spelling. Less sympathetic humanities teachers complain that we are not specialists and we therefore lack the professional knowledge to teach the subject. We make no claims to do either. We teach children. We aim to give our pupils the confidence to acquire the language skills they need to make sense of their world, their environment and their experience. We want them to enjoy their learning so that they want to learn more. We believe that, to quote a DES publication on the question,

> Remedial help in learning to read should wherever possible be closely related to the rest of a pupil's learning.[4]

and we are grateful to the Humanities Faculty for giving us ample opportunities for language development within their subject. We haven't got it right yet, but our pupils, in their own way, are helping us to get there.

Notes

1 BRUNER, J (1973) *The Relevance of Education*, New York, Wiley
2 FREIRE, P (1976) *Education, the Practice of Freedom*, London, Writers and Readers
3 THOMPSON, B (1979) *Reading Success*, London, Sidgwick
4 DEPARTMENT OF EDUCATION AND SCIENCE (1976) *A Language for Life* (The Bullock Report), London, HMSO

Developing a True Integrated
Humanities Syllabus

Ross Phillips

One difficulty in writing about integrated humanities is the problem of definition. In *The Humanities Jungle*, Anthony Adams acknowledged this problem before looking in detail at some humanities courses and projects.[1] Nevertheless there are many teachers who believe they know what integrated humanities is and are involved in its teaching. There are many schools with such courses and they have various titles.

I judge that an original model on which integrated humanities courses were based comes from projects such as the Schools Council Humanities Curriculum Project. Writing about this Project Stenhouse tried to pin down a definition when he wrote that

> we understand by the humanities they study of both human behaviour and human experience. The study of human behaviour is broadly the concern of social sciences: history, human geography, psychology and sociology.... The study of human experience is reflected in the arts and in the biographical aspect of history.[2]

Although thinking about integrated humanities has moved on since then, I believe this notion is useful since it illuminates some of the problems faced by teachers. It was important for many of us to establish courses which brought together a spectrum of separate subjects and disciplines in an attempt to provide an encounter with the complexity of human existence. Although the Humanities Curriculum Project was largely geared to 'the needs of adolescent pupils of average and below average ability', many schools, in Leicestershire at least, saw the need for such a course for *all* students and built them into their core curriculum.

Recent dissatisfaction with this area of work in schools needs to be explained and, looking back over the past decade, it is possible to see where the trouble started. The responsibility for some of these courses becoming sterile does not rest in any one quarter, there are a complex of reasons. Translating the ideals encapsulated in the humanities curriculum into the classroom was never going to be easy. It depended on more than goodwill, but few schools altered their appointments policy preferring to take on subject specialists first and humanities teachers second.

Bringing together teachers from diverse subject backgrounds with specialist concerns but a common commitment had the potential for lively innovation. In schools where humanities was seen as significant, there was a flourish of course development. Too often, however, even in the more enlightened schools which did not see humanities as a 'ROSLA' social studies course, the teachers who united have as their focus the social sciences. And too often these teachers sought to fight a corner in the course for their particular specialist input rather than starting from scratch and building something new, in the spirit of the enterprise. Rarely was the expressive and creative dimension of the humanities curriculum an essential, integral part of the design. In general, teachers' own training tended to reinforce the compartmentalization of knowledge.

Courses emerged which contained chunks of various existing social science syllabi. Where teachers were employed to work in this area, the advertisements were inevitably for teachers of 'social studies' which tended to encourage the domination of such courses by one or two perspectives. Apart from the problem of subject domination, teachers encountered difficulties with the classroom organization itself. There was a strong feeling that students should take responsibility for their own learning and pursue lines of enquiry which interested them. Students were to be active, engaged in the learning process and the classroom would be activity based.

Course development was being informed by a powerful trend in curriculum thinking. Denis Lawton and Barry Dufour's *The New Social Studies* opens with a chapter tracing the emergence of 'social studies' as an important component in the curriculum.[3] Although the book undoubtedly encourages both integration and active learning, it is interesting — twelve years on — to see how the 'social studies' movement nipped the growth of integrated humanities in the bud. Lawton and Dufour describe the influence of social science on the humanities curriculum and point out that a 'prevailing body of opinion ... subscribed to the view that social studies work ... would benefit from an increased reliance on content and method derived from the social sciences'.[4] Since many teachers coming into schools and into this area of

the curriculum were fresh from university and conscious of the importance of social science, it is no surprise that when constructing new
courses they drew heavily upon their own academic backgrounds.
Rejecting the previously held view that what was needed was a civics
course, teachers moved to the position that students needed a methodology based upon the objectivity social sciences then claimed to have.

The enthusiasm with which teachers created new courses is beyond
doubt. This enthusiasm also overcame a variety of problems. A deal of
excellent thinking and creativity took place. In many Leicestershire
upper schools a concern for most teachers is the world of examinations
and integrated humanities courses needed this seal of approval if they
were not to be seen as an adjunct to the curriculum. Squaring up to the
need for assessment meant that a learning process had to take place for
the teachers. Few of us had significant experience either in dealing with
examination boards or of methods of assessment. At the time the mode 3
facility seemed an obvious route as it offered hope of retaining control
over the syllabus and a mechanism which afforded a degree of flexibility
beyond a single, end of course, written paper. It was at this stage, in my
judgment, that the context in which we were working led to a mistake of
paramount importance. It was at this stage that the issue of what
integrated humanities is all about was fudged.

At the time, there was a naivety about what exam boards do. There
was little real understanding that the business of examining is not,
essentially, the same as the business of learning. Although it is
undoubtedly the case that some boards were helpful, they maintained
their traditional distance from the classroom experience and this was a
difficult fact to live with when the aspirations of the teachers included a
challenge to the typical form of assessing students. Approaching examination boards for mode 3 certificates highlighted some of the worst
aspects of the developments and concentrated thinking on assessment
rather than the learning process. The message received by the boards
suggested a demand for reasonably broad-based courses about society
drawing on the growth of academic interest and research in disciplines
such as sociology, economics and political science. There was no
mystery about this, there was no credibility problem since all the major
boards were expanding 'O' and 'A' level examinations in these subjects.

There were difficulties marrying up a course designed for the entire
ability range with the need to gain syllabus acceptance for CSE and 'O'
level. Often this required syllabuses to look different and it always
demanded rather different techniques of assessment. Nevertheless,
there was a surge of new, teacher-created syllabi, each one having local
variation but a familiar pattern. Lawton and Dufour include in their

book examples of these syllabi and local knowledge of Leicestershire schools submissions confirms the view that they were sequential and topic-based. The intention was to begin from an understanding of the individual as a social person moving on to a global awareness. Groby College's CSE world studies syllabus challenged this concept and Bosworth College had a joint English and social studies CSE syllabus. But by and large there is remarkable similarity in style and approach.

This is not surprising. Not only were we struggling with a difficult ideal, but also our own feelings of subject preciousness were hard to hold at bay. As teachers presented their arguments for such courses to the boards, and as they came to terms with the constraints of assessment, it was virtually inevitable that the syllabus would appear as a description of content rather than an explanation of a curriculum which was to be dynamic and embracing the spectrum that, for example, Stenhouse envisaged. A process having its roots in inadequate teacher training, employment policy and our academic consciousness was crystallized out in the syllabus document.

It is worth looking at the assessment of these courses in a little more detail. Exam boards have to be concerned with comparability, validity and reliability in methods of assessment since they are in the business of grading students' performance at the end of a two-year course and because they are accountable to public opinion for the annual results. Continuous assessment over two years is possible when all students follow the same route and are taught the same things. In submitting a syllabus based upon discrete units of knowledge, periodic, objective testing was made possible in terms of the boards' own criteria. Initial anxiety about mode 3 was soothed because social studies embodied the social sciences' contemporary hang-up about 'objectivity' and 'scientific' method. This ideology actually supported the view that this new aspect of the curriculum could be examined.

However, the failure to articulate that many courses integrated well beyond sociology, economics and political science had several implications. One consequence was that integrated humanities was pruned down to a *subject area* and for the purposes of examination interpreted as more or less equal to 'social studies'. Assessment procedures had as their focus tests of factual knowledge and weighed heavily on the classroom dynamic. It is inevitable that where the point of assessment is a test of something all students are understood to have encountered and remembered, the teacher will *predetermine* the process of discovery for the pupil. One aspect in the original idea — students pursuing their own line of enquiry — became difficult to manage since they might roam beyond the prescribed area of knowledge and thus cheat themselves out of a grade. Where a genuine attempt to include the area of human experience as revealed in the expressive arts was an integral part of the course, a separate syllabus with yet another assessment procedure had to run alongside.

A concession to the student-based enquiry dimension of these early initiatives was the acceptance of a major research project as a valid piece of assessable work. Again it is easy to see how such acceptance for exam purposes emphasized the assessment of *methodology* rather than the intrinsic experience involved in active investigation. Nevertheless, the 'project', which rarely attracted more than 20 per cent of the final marks, remains an important contribution. Yet teachers have found this problematic. Although they value the inclusion in the scheme of assessment of this component, they originally conceived it as an integral element of the *whole approach*, rather than a separately assessed entity. Given that 'social studies' demands the acquisition of structures and systems as factual knowledge, the 'project' has become something standing outside the central rationale of the course and the predominant experience in the classroom as perceived by the student is one of learning 'facts'. For an inexorable process has been at work which makes these courses increasingly 'taught'.

In 14–19 upper schools in Leicestershire, concern about end of course performance in the public examination system is ever-present. Although humanities teachers had been evaluating their contribution, trying to change and adapt, examination demands were never far from the surface of debate and always present in terms of defining tasks. It was nevertheless apparent five years ago when a group of teachers met to discuss the prospect of 16+ that despite a feeling about the burden of assessment, innovation *had* been taking place. This had, at minimum, taken the form of attempts to change or revise a syllabus, or moving to the then relatively new Joint Matriculation Board integrated humanities 'O' level syllabus. Although the group's main reason for meeting was concern about the future, discussion was wide-ranging and highlighted efforts to struggle beyond the constraints of self-imposed 'social studies' courses.

An example of one such development could be found at Bosworth College where, during the academic year 1980/81, discussions had taken place between design and humanities teachers. How possible is it for students in their final two years of compulsory school to experience their English, design and community studies education in one, integrated, course? What would be the consequences for students of working nine periods each week (one-and-a-half days) with teachers from both design and humanities departments working as a team? Initial feelings that the core courses offered in each faculty had some degree of overlap was an area to build on. By 1981 the idea had evolved that a timetable device could, for some students, bring together the two core areas of the curriculum in a new course.

Built into the concept of 'HUF' — the computer-coded title of the course which began in September 1981 — was the notion that students should organize their own time, work at their own pace and yet fulfil deadlines. Having rapidly rejected the regurgitation of traditional 'social studies' themes as a vehicle for integration, the teams were left with a desire to focus on skills, which proved an empty objective unless there was some indispensible factual content for students to manage. It was also clear that the course needed its own momentum and flow which encouraged students to be dynamic in the process rather than passive consumers. Permitting students to negotiate their own time caused bottlenecks, particularly at some stages of the design process when individual design teachers could be inundated with requests for help or materials. Humanities teachers gulped at the prospect of ninety lengthy essays to mark in one go. The team itself posed constraints, perhaps best illustrated by the need for teachers to possess a qualification and experience to work in a machine room. This tension between pedagogy and practicality persisted despite various attempts to find a solution, the most satisfactory of which was providing students with an eight-week diary of when lead lessons would be held and where. The 'content' versus 'skills' issue was resolved by opting for huge projects on, for example, a country such as Japan or China.

Although the availability of large chunks of time helped make this course a success, students were never totally the active agents in the process originally envisaged because the assessment procedures for five separate qualifications (CSE and 'O' level English, CSE and 'O' level social studies, CSE design) too often punctuated the experience by removing the student from this procedure at certain points. Even though expertise was developed in gearing work undertaken as part of an exploration of, say, China to a particular syllabus, it was a real pressure on the course. It meant chanelling interest away from its spontaneous beginnings to an investigation — sometimes less enthusiastically — of another issue, it stretched teachers to provide appropriate resources for assessment in areas not 'on stream' in the faculty resource bank and marking work became, at times, an overwhelming chore. Frequent team meetings were essential for the organization of the course, but discussion often concerned itself with the need for appropriate training for all those involved and, inevitably, anxiety about examination performance. Exam results were deemed to be only one facet of HUF's success or failure, but at the end of the first two-year cycle an analysis helped confidence. The pattern of entry for each examination varied, but overall achievement between HUF students and those following the more conventional core course route revealed differences and no more. Since rather more negotiation with students about which exams at what level was an aspect of HUF, differences were to be expected. No evidence of disadvantage could be detected. But there was little doubt that the fragmented nature of the examination requirements for HUF were a practical problem which a common examination at 16+ might help overcome.

The Leicestershire-based Integrated Humanities Coordinating Committee took on board this and many other experiences when deliberating about 16+. During the first round of responses to joint GCE/CSE proposals, the only syllabus remotely connected with the Leicestershire experience was that for social science which acknowledged integration to the extent that it utilized economics, sociology and political science. This original proposal, in a sense, celebrated the worst aspects of our own earlier submissions to examination boards and, as such, should have come as no surprise. From discussion about this, however, emerged the outline of an integrated humanities proposal which had as its focus the assessment of skills. Although the development of the syllabus has some way to go, Leicestershire teachers hope that the new Midlands Examining Group syllabus reflects the thinking and experience of the past five or more years. As the GCSE is introduced for humanities the hope is that assessment procedures will fit more harmoniously with the curriculum than they have perhaps done in the past.

However successful this teachers group has been in getting an integrated humanities syllabus off the ground and piloted amongst a dozen or so schools, and however pleased we may be that the Midland Examining Group are developing this syllabus for GCSE, it is really the experience of working together as teachers that has been the most valuable experience. For the GCSE will probably not be the end of the story as far as the humanities curriculum is concerned, and apart from debating assessment problems the group has proved an exceptional forum for identifying many other worries, sharing concerns and coming to terms with other new developments such as TVEI, CPVE and profiling approaches like those involved in OCEA. Assessing students is an aspect of teachers' work. There is a real need both for initial training and for in-service support to secure relevant and appropriate expertise for this area of the curriculum. It is vital that integrated humanities does not isolate itself from other developments and find itself out on a limb again.

Notes

1 ADAMS, A (1976) *The Humanities Jungle*, London, Ward Lock
2 From *Journal of Curriculum Studies*, 1, 1 (1969)
3 LAWTON, D and DUFOUR, B (1976) *The New Social Studies*, London, Heinemann
4 *Ibid*, p 14

The Story of a Syllabus

Lesley King

I trained as an integrated humanities teacher firstly because my degree in social science did not prepare me for any of the individual subjects then generally taught in schools, especially at lower secondary level, and secondly because I believed that learning must make more sense for students if they were able to use the concepts and skills of more than one subject, especially when exploring large and often complex issues. Later I taught integrated humanities in a situation flexible enough to facilitate individual and small group research of various kinds, one which allowed students to follow their own learning paths. So when I moved to a new school four years ago, it was natural for me to assume, with these past positive teaching and learning relationships in mind, that the careful development of the integrated humanities curriculum would be the way to develop the kind of environment in which students would gradually take control of their own learning with the positive support of their teachers.

This piece of writing charts my experience at the school, and highlights the dangers of concentrating on curriculum and syllabus at the expense of more basic school organization. The 'integrated humanities' we developed became a traditionally-taught school 'subject' like any other, albeit bigger, better resourced and more popular than some. The full realization of this came for me when a colleague asked me in the staffroom what he was supposed to be teaching that week — and I told him! Integrated humanities, like English, can have advantages over other subjects in the school curriculum. Its subject matter often has an immediate appeal to students, and they can bring their own opinions, interests and experiences to bear on their learning. The longer periods often allowed for it on the timetable can give rise to a variety of approaches denied to other subjects, and can lead to a closer working relationship between teacher and student than is usual. But if we are not careful we can just teach more *factual content* in a more efficient manner than teachers of other subjects, while deluding ourselves that we have transformed the learning environment in some significant way. This is what happened to me.

I went to the school in 1981 as head of lower school. The school was an 11–18 comprehensive with approximately 1000 students on roll. It was on two sites with a mile between them. The lower school, which housed the first two years, (nearly 400 students aged 11–13 years) was based in the former grammar school buildings just outside the town. Most teachers taught on the two sites although I and one or two others were based entirely at the lower school.

Integrated studies was already taught in the lower school only, as a combination of history, geography and religious education to mixed ability classes in the first year and to set groups in the second. It was supervised by the heads of history and geography who were based at the upper school. They shared teaching groups at the lower school with other integrated studies teachers for two hours each a week to check how things were going. They had been largely instrumental in devising the syllabus several years previously. All other teachers teaching integrated studies were form tutors at the lower school but had other commitments at the upper school too. The first year syllabus was based on a study of the local area using a carefully researched school-produced work book. The second year syllabus, as far as I could gather, ran from 'early man' to the 'industrial revolution', or further if there was time, with a long stop over at 'the Tudors'. Resources for all this (except for the Tudors) were in short supply. There was only one regular field day for the second year students, looking at geographical and historical features of the Cotswolds, although the first year course involved research in the local community.

This was the area I was to work in, and although my job involved a good deal more than the coordination of the integrated humanities programme, I was optimistic that developments and changes here could gradually effect the learning environment of the lower school. But, of course, there were quite serious early constraints.

The school had a very strong departmental structure and the heads of department guarded their terrain carefully. There was very little philosophical support for the integration of subjects. The heads of history and geography expressed strong reservations about the spread of integrated studies into the third year, and when they taught at lower school they tended to teach historical and geographical aspects of the course respectively, because that is where their confidence and expertise lay. There was no such thing as an integrated studies *department*. Certain geography and history teachers taught integrated studies at the lower school leaving me without a department to relate to at first. I sensed two major worries about my intervention from the outset. There was a feeling that I might want to see integrated studies as more than the sum of the three subjects so far combined. This was true of course. There was also a mistaken feeling that I might want to jettison everything so far developed, replacing it with a course firmly based on sociology or worse! Obviously, therefore, there was no sense that the development of integrated humanities would have support form senior staff.

Another constraint, was the physical environment of the teaching area, which was drably austere. The set of classrooms used for integrated studies was furnished with ill-assorted old desks and chairs. They led into the lower school's largish practical and resources area, with a television room, balcony and library. These were dreary but had potential (except for the balcony, which a cleaner informed me was used for sixth-form spitting contests in the old grammar school days).

The resources were also in a mess, the fossils of a vanished curriculum. Deep down many text books survived from the old selective era including some I had never really believed existed, glorifying the Empire and castigating 'savages'. St Paul's journeys were regularly retraced. Dust gathered on time-charts of British kings and queens. Half-finished models of medieval castles were propped up in corners surrounded by old subbuteo boards, almost-working gas masks and aged coconuts in their outer shells. Tattered posters from the RSPCA, the Post Office and Shell Mex, broken thermometers and rusty rain gauges all shared cupboards with old examination paper (95 per cent factual recall, 5 per cent map work). Glass slides of an unknown city and newer slides of school trips to London and Stonehenge were hidden under relics of the Great Western Railway. Maps of the world made of oil cloth and strung on poles showed the position of the Belgian Congo and Tanganyika, while encyclopaedias contained all the latest news about Rutland and Rhodesia. These same encyclopaedias informed us that there were three separate races of mankind usually known as black, white and yellow, although Christianity was often useful in uniting them. The top layer held more recent and rather rakish posters from Friends of the Earth and CND, and piles of bandas, none of which revealed a full-blooded attempt at building up a viable resources bank.

I taught a first year mixed-ability group of thirty-three and a second year top set of thirty-five. Other teachers in the area were welcoming but rushed. All needed to dash from site to site leaving me to dig for outline maps of Great Britain and textbooks on 'early man' which hadn't been furnished with suggestive annotation by former readers. My classes were slightly rowdy in that way that classes are if you have neither committed compulsory material to memory, nor are you committed to that material. The nadir came when I drew a diagrammatic representation of the early verses of Genesis on the blackboard using a work sheet borrowed from another school, and a box of multi-coloured chalks. Everyone copied it carefully into their books. The silence that comes from busy work! It was only much later that I realized that when God was resting on the seventh day in the original, he was still busy creating man and woman in my version. I couldn't summon the energy to own up.

But things began to change. Two integrated studies teachers left at the end of year, one to practise self-sufficiency, another to teach geography at another school. To my regret, a third decided to accompany her class to the upper school and concentrate on the teaching of history. The journey between two sites on a moped had proved too much. The new appointments brought vitality and freshness to the job in hand. Two of them were keen to work entirely at the lower school. One was a primary-trained historian, the other a geographer with interest in, and experience of, teaching integrated humanities. The third appointment was to teach half-time in integrated studies and half-time in economics at the upper school. The new group was completed by another full-time lower school tutor already teaching English and music, a deputy head who would teach one group and myself on a half timetable. The group which would work on the integrated studies curriculum during the next two years consisted of these six teachers plus the heads of geography and history who no longer taught at the lower school but maintained an interest. Another important appointment came at about the same time. The lower school librarian left to work in a travel agency, and was replaced by the upper school librarian, a woman of boundless energy and enthusiasm who agreed to run the library and help to organize the resources at the lower school.

I was still certain that the most valuable learning takes place when the school structure allows students and teachers to work together in an open-ended and flexible way, with the time and space to develop working relationships where the students' interests, talents, views and questions would inform the work in hand. I was still optimistic that this way of working could be developed within integrated studies and from there begin to influence work throughout the lower school.

So how was this new group of teachers to work together? I could have insisted that we follow my ideas. But two of the teachers were probationers and others far from convinced of the validity of such views. There was no model in the school to learn from, so induction in that way was not possible. Furthermore I was committed to working in a democratic way with the group, replicating as far as I could the kind of classroom relationships that I was advocating. We would learn from each other as we worked together. With the full cooperation of the head, some decisions were made immediately. Setting was stopped, and we began work simultaneously on improving the learning environment and updating the resources. With some of us teaching it for the first time, we decided to assess the syllabus as we taught it, in order to work together on its development at a later stage, when we had all settled into our jobs.

Work started at once. Tables gradually replaced the old desks, some of which were burned, others sold to parents. We borrowed tables from the dining hall, from behind the stage, from the upper school and from the primary school down the road then moving to new premises. We sold old pine and oak cupboards, teachers' desks and specimen cabinets. Antique dealers counted used £1 notes into the secretary's nervous hands and tables were bought with the proceeds. The head bought others with furniture capitation. The rarely used chairs stacked on the stage gradually replaced the old ones. Children sat on the floor during assemblies and could bring their chairs to the hall when they were needed for parents' meetings and productions. The caretaker put up more noticeboards and they were quickly used for the display of students' work and for other stimulus material, as well as for form notice boards. Large woodwork tables rejected by another school soon filled the practical room, while dustbins requisitioned by the caretaker now held all the odds and ends that are needed for practical work — though some cleaners did insist right to the end on emptying their hoovers into them. No doubt some zealous students used that dust for their models of iron age settlements. We ordered great quantities of painting materials and stored them in an old wardrobe bought from the caretaker for £5 including delivery. The television room was organized for easy showing of slides, films and videos and for small group taping. The balcony was permanently locked. Next came the library. Huge carelles were moved out into the classrooms for display purposes, leaving it a light and airy room. Curtains, bought at a jumble sale were adapted by the librarian to fit the huge windows. Parents paid for comfortable seating to comple- ment the chairs and tables already present. Eventually the whole top floor was painted and some rooms carpeted. All this work was important for several reasons. Firstly, teachers and students have a right to work in pleasant surroundings. Secondly, if the area is well-organized and attractive you gain credibility with other members of staff who are perhaps, not immediately attracted to your philosophy, and it raises the morale of those that are. Thirdly, students work better in aesthetically pleasing and well-organized surroundings. They need to be part of a purposeful and workmanlike atmosphere. They need to know where the scissors and glue are. They need resources to be available before the enthusiasm wanes and, most importantly, an orderly area means that there is more time for conversations between teacher and students, and student and student.

Our review of the books in the library and resources area went on. Redundant books were sent to jumble sales, Sunday schools or burned. Children even bought, for 3p each, tattered copies of *Heroes of the Old Testament*, or *The Boys' Book of Things to Do*, containing instructions for making a periscope in order to see the Coronation. A rumour went round the community that we were Bible burning. Gradually the library was restocked by purchase and more county loans than I have every seen gathered in one place before. After the bonfires, which had become a regular feature behind the caretaker's bungalow, after we had emptied every cupboard, thrown out paper resources or distributed them elsewhere, the librarian catalogued what was left and began a film, slide and video catalogue, the kernel of the new resources area.

While all this was going on we began to discuss the integrated studies syllabus. I might have been tempted to destroy everything, but we decided to adapt what we had. Some elements of the syllabus seemed to be working well and we had neither the time, energy or money to start from scratch in our first year together. We did agree that the syllabus was much too big, leading to superficial coverage of too many areas, and encouraging a passive mode of learning and didactic teaching. So, fairly ruthless cuts were made and we decided on a basic outline of possible work and the preparation of resources began.

The guiding principle of this time was that we should work closely together and share our ideas. New paper resources were displayed on a board in the TV room which also contained news of relevant films, slides and videos. Ideas for lessons themselves were shared at a regular series of informal meetings, and as we did not work in closed classrooms, we learned from each other as we went along. We had time too to plan together and reflect together formally and informally. We talked particularly of skills we hoped to develop and shared ideas for practical activities — a weather station, making fire without matches, hot air balloons, flint arrowheads, scale models, designing inventions to increase man's agility and brain power, jigsaws of continental drift and reconstructions of local architectural features. We encouraged children to bring in their own resources like family treasures and we directed them into the local community to observe, interview and chat. We invited members of the community to visit us too to share their experiences and specialized knowledge. More field trips were arranged.

The syllabus arose out of what was there, what we felt had gone well, what *we* thought was valuable and what we knew was available elsewhere. It seemed fairly coherent and at the end of our second year we were ready to write down a tentative version of our aims and the syllabus itself, although as we wrote they changed still.

One of the main aims of our course was that students enjoyed work in the area and left us interested in the world around them and eager to find out and understand more. More specific aims included the shared responsibility for the teaching of basic skills which should underpin much of student learning. These range from careful observation to a personal exploration of ideas, issues and situations by creative and expressive means of various kinds. Creative learning was encouraged wherever possible. We recognized also our special responsibility for introducing the skills generally thought of as the province of the historian and geographer which were needed to facilitate students' progress further up the school. We hoped too that they would explore the spiritual element in peoples' lives and be able to reflect on their own beliefs alone and with others. We hoped to encourage the personal characteristics of self-discipline, independent initiative and confidence in their own ideas and opinions. On the other hand, we hoped students would develop the confidence to doubt, and to accept that not all questions have easy answers, permanent answers or even answers at all. We did not wish to merely inculcate facts, recognizing that rote learning is not just a low-level learning activity but also promotes certainty when there is often none. We tried to encourage a more tentative approach. Lastly we hoped to encourage children to work cooperatively, learning from one another and respecting each others' opinions and ideas. We accepted that some of our aims were linked together and found it difficult to write them down in water-tight compartments. They syllabus itself follows.

First Year
  1 Myself
  2 My family
  3 Where I live (from the local area to the solar system!)
  4 The weather
  5 Studies in the locality.

In the second year we went right back to the beginning of life on earth. The work dealt with more abstract issues, and there were less likely to be straightforward answers to the questions posed by the children.

Second Year
1 In the beginning (The beginning of earth and early life)
2 The coming of man
3 Hunting and gathering
4 The coming of farming and its effects.

All the above were based on the excellent BBC *Man* Radiovision programmes.

5 One World — Britain and the West Indies based on *One World*, the BBC's school videos reflecting the ideas in the Brandt Report.
6 The development of Bristol (based on ITV's school videos *Manscape*).

We had different justifications for the inclusion of each of these eleven areas. For instance, a study of 'myself' seemed particularly appropriate as children came into the school from thirteen different primary schools. They shared knowledge about themselves with each other and we began to know them personally. This was vital if we were to work together as a group. Secondly we were anxious that children did not start work in our area with the belief that all valuable knowledge and ideas came from books or from teachers. Thirdly, the theme lent itself easily to all kinds of practical activities such as modelling, painting, role play, conversations and discussions. Writing that students were involved in tended to be personal and reflective, rather than merely writing to record. So we hoped that students would realize, right from the outset, that we valued work which was an expression of their own ideas and feelings and that we did not elevate factual note-taking above other ways of working.

Other areas of study had more specific aims. For instance we looked at Britain and the West Indies as an aspect of multicultural education. We examined the welfare gaps between countries of the North-South divide, looked at processes of change in the two countries and the interdependence we share. We tried to avoid showing developing countries as places entirely taken up with disasters, hoping to show achievements and enjoyment of life too. We tried also to avoid a touristic approach by concentrating on one area in depth, rather than looking at the exotic or peculiar across the developing world, and we tried to direct students to particular issues rather than encourage them to acquire too many facts. This then was a very direct attempt at encouraging students to understand and to develop empathy with people from another culture connected to our own.

We had achieved a lot in two-and-a-half years. Some aspects of the development pleased me well. Firstly and most importantly, everyone concerned (teachers and librarian) had worked together over a long period learning from each other in the face of a shared task. I learnt a lot and my teaching was enriched by the experience. I was fortunate to have been part of the group. In the course of our work we had transformed the physical environment and had built up an impressive array of resources ranging from textbooks, county collections, paper resources prepared nationally or by us, short stories, poems, novels, audio-visual aids of all kinds, and artefacts, to the experience of families and friends, to people in the community and the locality. We had managed to vary our ways of working from teacher exposition, to individual and small group research and practical activities. We had tried to emphasize that although factual writing plays an important part in childrens' work in the area, we saw conversation, discussion, graphic work and creative work of all kinds as vital routes to learning too. We began to prove that large and complex issues such as 'what makes me human' could be tackled when we were allowed to cross subject boundaries. What is more, students did begin to see that there wasn't a 'correct' answer to every question they asked, and, in my view they did begin to respect each others ideas and opinions more as they tackled such issues as the beginning of the world, personal religious beliefs and the rights and duties of mankind towards other animals.

We teachers grew confident enough not to integrate our subjects for integration's sake. We didn't study 'Weather in the Bible' for instance! Some of our themes were almost entirely historical, some had a strong geographical bias. On the other hand we knew that integrated humanities was more than a combination of history, geography and religious education. For example, in a study of the local abbey which had become the town's parish church we hoped that, while working in our area, children would make personal and creative responses and aesthetic judgments which might traditionally concern the English teacher and the art teacher.

Three of us followed the logic of the view that the centre of any study was not the subject but the student, who should be helped to respond to concern in any appropriate way unhindered by subject boundaries. We began to teach English to the same groups we already saw for integrated studies. We halved the number of children we worked with in the week and increased our flexibility enormously. Two of us were also tutors, allowing us a gradual blend of our pastoral and academic role. So the responsibility for a larger area of the curriculum was a positive step for all of us. Now we saw children up to ten hours a week out of twenty four, and the quality of students' work was improved, as we got to know each other better. Not that English and integrated studies were always combined in our work of course. We were conscious that students needed room for creative self-expression which is not related to a theme and reading which is purely for pleasure, and reading to which the response is sometimes more specific, some-times more wide-ranging than a thematic approach might give. Even so I remember with pleasure times when the subjects did come together in a natural way, as they did once when we were looking at early man's harnessing of fire with our attempts at creating fire ourselves with home made fire drills, our speculation on how fire might have been subju-gated and then made at will, our reading from Jack London on the vital importance of being able to light a fire on the Yukon trail and the powerful poems written by some students describing the moment of exultation felt by man when he realized that the power of fire was his. So the inclusion of English undeniably helped our work and gave more meaning to a syllabus already coherent to many students. It was flexible enough to allow some choice and to suit mixed ability classes. It allowed us all to introduce ideas and concepts that we felt were important, and on the whole it was generally popular with our students, as their attitude and the standard of their work suggested.

In many ways integrated studies was a great success due to an enthusiastic, energetic and talented group of people and to the support and cooperation of the head. Why wasn't I satisfied then? Why didn't I stay to refine the work done in the area and to enlarge its scope? I had hoped that integrated studies would create the conditions necessary for students to begin to take control of their own learning. Even when combined with English, however, integrated humanities remained a traditional secondary school subject like any other even though it was carefully thought out, well resourced, employed a variety of working methods, paid due regard to skills as well as content, was enthusiastical-ly taught, and in the main very well received by students. The work was still mainly teacher-directed throughout the two years as I suspect most integrated humanities work is. Whether we think children should learn about their origins, other cultures, or explore the causes of social problems, our classrooms reflect almost entirely our views on what is good for children. My own prejudices are quite apparent in our syllabus. What is more we teachers usually had the upper hand, normally possessing superior knowledge, control of the resources, and were more articulate. We lacked the time or will to listen and respond to students' needs. So when a boy wanted to do more research on an exciting set of family photographs he had brought in, I did not work with him long enough and his enthusiasm waned. If he had persevered, he would have missed all the work on mapping anyway, which I knew was necessary for his geography classes in the third year. So I steered him onto work on the Ordnance Survey map of his area, where resources were plentiful and I had the answers to any question he might pose. Once again what I felt was important took precedence and I believe his real education suffered accordingly.

There are equal dangers in the opposite view. I remember Jan Mark's horrific chapter about a secondary school classroom in her novel *Thunder and Lightning*, where one of the boys had 'done fish' for several years as his project and most of the girls 'did horses'. One boy excelled himself by 'doing Tarzan' because all you had to do was cut him out and stick him in. 'Why not do worms then?', said the new boy as a joke. 'Worms are easy!' And one of the members of the class sat down to give the idea serious consideration. I am not suggesting that teachers give up their role altogether, as the shadowy figure in charge of that classroom obviously had. I am looking for a more reciprocal relationship between teacher and student. So when a second year girl accused me of being cranky about the Bushmen of the Kalahari Desert, I should have had the time to explain to her why I felt they were an important area of study, and she should have felt the freedom to reject my opinions and opt for something else if she chose. And she should have felt confident enough in our working relationship to listen to my views on her choice of work, and be able to reject or accept them from a position of equality. And then if she had decided to persevere with her area of study I should have had the time and other resources to help her. Instead I carried her along more or less with my enthusiasm for the topic I felt was important and had so carefully prepared. This is a viable mode of teaching but it should not be employed constantly at the expense of a more interactive one.

Why did we never reach that stage in integrated studies? Firstly, we had not paid enough attention to timetable and classroom organization which allows the individual conversations with students out of which reciprocal work arises. Our lessons were scattered throughout the week. Work on one theme ended at a particular time and a new theme followed, often dependent on a major film booked for a particular date. Individual and small group research took place within carefully pre-scribed limits. So it was inevitable that members of our classes were all busy at the same time not needing us, while they ended their work at roughly the same time too, making individual and small group conversations and discussions impossible to arrange. We moved through the syllabus together along a route planned in advance, with extra work for the quick and keen student and extra attention, if possible, for the slow learner.

Perhaps we would have discussed our classroom organization more if we had not thought our syllabus was so important. Paradoxically, our enthusiastic hard work together had committed us too heavily to our course, and this enthusiasm and the very variety of our resources and ideas arising from it had squeezed out student's ideas from serious consideration. And my commitment to working together in a democratic way in the group, moving forward only when consensus was reached, militated against any dilution of the syllabus. There was no sign that any member of the group was ready to take the risks involved in moving away from our course despite all the creative ways we had developed to move through it.

A further stumbling block of course was that we did not have the energy to diversify our resources enough to cope with the encouragement of student autonomy. No one department could develop the kind of resource centre needed if students are to be encouraged to follow up their own ideas and interests as well as follow paths planned by teachers in advance. There was no teacher in charge of resources in the school, and no need for one perceived. The development of resources was seen as the job of each department to fit in with their scheme of work.

One single department cannot provide the skills and expertise needed to facilitate students' control of their own learning. The whole school, and above all, the departmental structure in which we feel so secure, needs to make the decision to put students at the centre of their organization. And the organization needs to allow for teachers with different expertise and interests to work together so that they can enlarge and develop their own skills in order to rise to a more demanding situation.

There was no hope of that decision being reached at my last school. Indeed the departments were so strong that there was no attempt even to coordinate the curriculum we served up to students who soon got used to psychedelic bursts of teaching on unrelated subjects. This is true of many secondary schools of course. If there was no general support for the coordination of the curriculum, there was certainly not going to be any philosophical support for the integration of subjects necessary if time and space are to be found so that individual students' wishes and needs can be given serious consideration.

The third year remained firmly divided into separate subjects with separate teachers. Integrated studies was praised at the lower school but was seen as a junior form of organization. It was all right in its place until the *serious business* of education began. Even at the lower school there was still a lot of distrust about integration. English teachers saw us taking over their territory when our work was not entirely factual. For instance, there were complaints over our work on 'myself' and 'the seasons', and when we used poems and short stories and personal writing to explore ideas and opinions. The fact that three of us also taught English did not help. The idea of a longer period with one teacher was not seen to be a good idea. 'Secondary students like plenty of teachers', some said, even though those students still saw at least eight teachers throughout the week. 'What if they are stuck with a poor teacher?' others said. They had different reservations too with this, the strongest 'I hope you've got English qualifications', or at best, 'Well of course *you* can do it, but you cannot expect anyone else to manage it. It's too difficult for most teachers to teach more than one subject.' These criticisms implied that teachers had reached the end of their develop- ment and did not allow for the exciting opportunities for continued learning from each other that a new organization might allow. All this too, when English teachers have always had the prerogative to teach anything they wanted, even in the most traditional schools, be it debating apartheid or bloodsports, issuing questionnaires on smoking or unemployment, discussing whether there is life after death or supervis- ing projects on dinosaurs or Henry VIII!

Other departments complained about our poaching of subject matter — evolution, air pressure, block graphs, self-portraits. More importantly a few children themselves complained about repetition and inconsistencies in their work. This lack of coherence, this subject exclusiveness and repetition which is not reinforcement, posed impor- tant philosophical and pragmatic problems, and the more successful we were at allowing students to follow their own learning paths, the more problems such as these would have arisen. I was not keen to meet and discuss the situation as I felt that meetings would only have served to erect stronger barriers between subjects than existed already, for such was the strength of departmental feeling in the school. Even when individual teachers were keen to help as was the 3-D specialist, they were normally overworked already. We hesitated to send students with their life-sized figures of Roman soldiers down to the workshop when he was already supervising sixteen students on the bandsaw.

So I gradually realized that the kind of learning environment I was aiming for was not a possibility. If, in the short term we as a department were too committed to our new and successful course to find the time or energy or even the will to give real consideration to students' needs and wishes, perhaps, this was a necessary learning phase. Perhaps we need the security of a syllabus at first. Perhaps we need to feel pride in a well-worked-out course before we are ready to relax a little and take the kind of risks implied in sharing the uncertainty of exploring unknown areas with students. Then as we enjoy the satisfaction of mutual discovery we gradually find it easier until an equal working relationship is developed. We might have worked in this way eventually, but we would not have solved the real problem. The school itself was still dominated by a departmental structure and was likely to remain so. If students are to follow their own learning paths, they need to be able to break through all subject boundaries and call upon any relevant expertise whenever needed. There was no possibility that the school would be organized to allow this to happen.

I am still a committed integrated humanities teacher. The integration of subjects is necessary if the time, space and flexibility is to be found for students' own concern to be followed through. Furthermore the study of humanities, especially when English is included, is well suited to the kind of work which can arise from a reciprocal working relationship, involving students as it often does in an intense and personal way. But I know also that integrated humanities, however successful, can be as teacher-dominated as any traditional school 'subject'. We need to develop the confidence to be able to jettison our syllabuses when appropriate, and we need to make sure that our classroom organization allows for the individual voice. Even then, we have to accept that no one group of people with similar expertise and experience can fulfil our students' raised expectations of us. We need to work towards a *whole-school* agreement on the principle that the student should be central to the learning process and towards something more than a departmental organization to allow this principle to be translated into reality, towards an organization which allows teachers with different strengths to learn from each other, to use each other's skills in order to help the students reach their goals.

Meanwhile I expect that my information sheets on the Bushman are working their way down the dusty layers of the integrated studies resources, waiting to be discovered and rejected by the next group of teachers working on a new humanities syllabus.

The Process Model of Integrated Humanities: Some Principles of Work in the Early Secondary Years

Jim Greany and Derek Francis

Integrated humanities takes many different forms according to the particular requirements and characteristics of each situation in which it has been introduced. There are schemes in which integrated humanities programmes are based on very careful structuring by the teacher or teachers concerned, of both the content of the programme and its methods; there are others in which almost complete freedom of choice in matters of content is given to each individual child, often within related areas centred on a common theme. In some cases, this kind of development has been associated with some form of team-teaching and thus with the combined working of several classes together; in others it is handled by individual teachers adopting a 'generalist' approach with one class. Sometimes the methods adopted have been largely heuristic with pupils encouraged to explore and 'find out for themselves' or 'learn by discovery'; on the other hand, often a directly didactic or instructional approach has been used. There are also many variations in the range and type of subjects included under the integrated humanities umbrella depending again on the purposes of the teacher or teachers involved and even on individual preferences — some schools just integrate history, geography and social studies, others add religious education, some include English and some even aspects of design. There are in fact so many variables that generalization becomes a very difficult task and teachers, especially in the early secondary range, have enjoyed a great deal of freedom in planning integrated humanities, liberated as they are from the usual examination strictures. Despite this variance there are, nevertheless, characteristics common to all approaches. It is these essential elements of integrated humanities which we hope to develop in this chapter.

The underlying aims and objectives of an integrated humanities course are to be found within the realms of Stenhouse's 'process model' and Esner's 'expressive objectives' and are far removed from the prescriptive narrow behavioural confines of Bloom's 'taxonomy'. Essentially, integrated humanities draws together skills and concepts and focusses on the process of their acquisition. This harks back to Jerome Bruner's statement in 1966:

> A body of knowledge, enshrined in a university faculty and embodied in a series of authoritative volumes, is the result of much prior intellectual activity. To instruct someone in these disciplines is not a matter of getting him to commit results to mind. Rather, it is to teach him to participate in the process that makes possible the establishment of knowledge. We teach a subject not to produce little living libraries on that subject but rather to get a student to think mathematically for himself, to consider matters as an historian does, to take part in the process of knowledge getting. Knowledge is a process not a product.[1]

In essence, Bruner's aim in *Man: A Course of Study* was not to 'get across' a particular course content, but to develop the powers of the learners. As he says in *The Relevance of Education*:

> The more elementary a course and the younger its students, the more serious must be its pedagogical aim of forming the intellectual powers of those whom it serves.[2]

For him, then, the aims of fostering cognitive growth precede selection of content. This is a very different approach from the more conventional one which would specify the content of a curriculum that the children should be expected to learn by a given age or stage. He is more concerned with skills, processes and attitudes than with facts for their own sake. Not that facts are not important: skills cannot be learned in the absence of experiences and materials; but which facts and experiences should be selected depends on their power to develop cognitive growth.

Like Bruner, Vygotsky believed in a systematic structure to learning. Child-centred programmes which focus purely on the 'spontaneous concepts' of students would have been anathema to him. Commenting on Ach's experiments, Vygotsky says they 'take into account that a concept is not an isolated, ossified changeless formation but an active part of the intellectual process constantly engaged in serving communication understanding and problem solving'. Through his research on egocentric speech Vygotsky demonstrated how in early childhood concept (complex) development and the child's dealings with the real world are inextricably linked.

> Our experiments brought to the fore another important point overlooked so far; the role of the child's activity in the evolution of his thought processes. We have seen that egocentric speech is not suspended in a void but is directly related to the child's practical dealings with the real world. We have seen that it enters as a constituent part into the process of rational activity, taking on intelligence as it were from the child's incipiently purposeful actions and that it increasingly serves problem solving and planning as the child's activities grow more complex. This process is set in motion by the child's actions; the objects he deals with mean reality and shape his thought processes.[3]

To Vygotsky concept formation is a 'creative not a mechanical passive process' and the 'mere presence of external conditions favouring a mechanical linking of word and object does not suffice to produce a concept'. The implications of Vygotsky's views are to see learning as both an intensely social and intensely personal process. A conceptual framework should be seen as a set of organizing ideas or principles which do not have to be slavishly followed or accepted. Concepts are tentative, speculative, notions that only exist in as much as they are held to exist by people at any particular point in time. In many schools the concepts of the academic 'disciplines' are viewed as though carved in tablets of stone.

The tablets-of-stone view is not however confined to traditionally taught subjects. Some teachers of concept-based curriculum see concepts as sacred keys to learning which must be grasped before progress is made. That these teachers have missed something is pointed out by Lawrence Stenhouse in an essay entitled 'The process model':

> Within knowledge and art areas, it is possible to select content for a curriculum unit without reference to student behaviours or indeed to ends of any kind other than that of representing the form of knowledge in the curriculum. This is because a form of knowledge has structure, and it involves procedures, concepts and criteria. Content can be selected to exemplify the most important procedures, the key concepts and the areas and situations in which the criteria hold.
>
> Now it might be thought that this is to designate procedures, concepts and criteria as objectives to be learned by the students. This strategy could, of course, be followed but it would

I believe distort the curriculum. For the key procedures, concepts and criteria in any subject — course form, experiment, tragedy — are, and are important precisely because they are, problematic within the subject. They are the focus of speculation, not the object of mastery.[4]

John Dewey too agreed with the ideas of process rather than product when he wrote on the distinction between thinking and thought:

Thinking is an active, vital dynamic process full of natural excitement and wonder involving the constant testing of hypotheses. Thought on the other hand is the end of the process, both its fruit and its termination unless of course thought gives rise to another chain of thinking. Much of what is represented by aims and objectives is thought. The result of other peoples challenges and struggles. Not surprisingly much of the excitement has been lost, the thinking eliminated and learners asked to store other people's harvest.[5]

In *Beyond Curriculum* Doug Holly examines in detail the ideas of Bruner and Vygotsky and develops his own thesis:

Whatever subject matter schools do or do not teach they must have regard to process; particularly they must be concerned with developing the systematic language of consciousness. Starting with the spontaneous meanings developed in the ordinary way by simply growing up in a given human society, organized education is about the systematic encouragement of self-conscious ideas, meanings which enable men and women to take a full part in the determination of their own destiny — the extension of democracy in educational terms.[6]

One of the fundamental differences between integrated humanities and a more traditional approach is the emphasis placed on defining and utilizing the skills involved in the learning activity as opposed to establishing the content of the various courses. Particular skills will of course be decided on according to locational factors such as the expertise of the staff, the interests of the learners and the availability of resources. An exhaustive, prescriptive list would be somewhat anti-thematic. Below, however, are some of the skills developed in courses for younger secondary pupils in which the authors have been involved:

Question posing	Evaluating evidence
Hypothesizing	Role playing

Observing	Presenting through a variety of media
Interpreting	Empathizing
Listening	Researching
Discussing	Cooperating

These skills have been developed within a structured and ordered environment that is characterized by the range of activities that students engage in. On a not atypical afternoon one could expect to find students:

Working in groups or alone, on investigative projects;

Walking to and fro to the resources base;

Discussing work with peers and/or teachers;

Listening in groups or classes to teachers leading stimulus or concept sessions;

Viewing, either in classes or small groups, slides, videos or film;

Making models, painting or working on socio-drama scenes;

Using computers;

Making tapes;

Mounting work;

Working quietly on written work;

Using first-hand artifacts or facsimilies provided by the museum service;

Working outside the building or otherwise making something.

(We might add here that when students have any spare time they sit polishing their halos.) Now of course things go wrong; at times it's too messy and at times it's too noisy, but generally it works very well. Presentation is often very good as students view the work as arising intrinsically from their relationship with the environment and from what they feel is important. Two things of course are vital: firstly relationships must be humanistic, and secondly there must exist a genuine spirit of enquiry.

According to Richard Pring

At certain stages of schooling, the process of enquiry (learning how to articulate the problem, how to formulate a hypothesis, how to find evidence etc) is more important than the product. The logical ordering of subject matter that the teacher is familiar with is the result of the unitary process of enquiry. It is not to be presented as such to the pupil, but is to be treated as a useful resource and guideline in helping the pupil with his enquiry into his problem — the enquiry that he finds of value.[7]

Enquiry-based learning is fundamental to integrated humanities and any syllabus worth its salt must include practice in the skills of individual and group enquiry. Locating, selecting, extracting and recording information from a wide range of different sources and using appropriate research methods and distinguishing that which should count as relevant evidence are all vital skills in making sense of perceived reality. Learning how to learn must pre-suppose learning what to learn. The narrow single-subject approach at best views this the other way round; at worst views only the latter.

Underpinning all this, say Moore and Lawson, is clearly a much wider view of education than the more conventional one.

> Education in any normative sense of the term involves initiating pupils into various aspects of knowledge, understanding and skill. This must involve the pupil in learning something, coming to understand what he is taught. Now no one can be initiated into anything unless he actively takes part in the initiating proceedings. This participation is the business of being educated. Participation involves a sharing in an enterprise, with others, taking one's part and knowing that one is doing so. So participation in the business of learning, trying to come to understand, is a necessary condition of being educated. Pupils must participate in this sense or education isn't taking place at all.[8]

It follows that in engaging in independent resource-based enquiry and analysis the relationship of teacher/learner must clearly be affected. How? Conventionally the role of the teacher in the classroom is that of the superior authority in a particular subject area. He/she is the one with right subject knowledge in the classroom of the ignorant. The uncompromising transmission of information, which is mistakenly what defines education in the conventional classroom, is always in the control of the teacher and the captive consumers are fed the product uncritically. So what happens if the learner is allowed some control? Does this mean that the teacher becomes unimportant or even unnecessary? Obviously not. What we have with the less conventional integrated humanities approach is not only a different more active role for the learner but also a different — and more active — role for the teacher.

In this, teachers are less distant from the pupils and their relationship is more interpersonal. The extent of their authority depends far more on their expertise not only in a subject area or areas but in a wide range of pedagogical abilities. These include their ability to organize pupils' work, to advise them on many aspects of it, to help them to frame their questions rather than merely to provide definitive answers, to make sure the learners are stretched while steering them away from work of a level that would be likely to defeat them, to provide opportunities for Bruner's 'enactive learning' to take place, and to develop the kinds of interpersonal relationship that will both forward the pupil's learning and establish the teacher's right to direct it.

Adopting enquiry-based learning as an integral part of integrated humanities is thus no soft option for the teacher — or the learner — as Lawrence Stenhouse points out in his essay

> the teacher needs some hold on, and a continual refinement of, a philosophical understanding of the subject he is teaching and learning, of its deep structures and their rationale. The teacher needs to take on to his agenda a desire to understand the nature of social science, the value problems it raises and its relation to the questions at the centre of the course. Only when he has gone some way towards structuring his own understanding of these issues can he adopt the pedagogy of the course.[9]

Surely what we are aiming for in an integrated humanities approach to teaching and learning is a shift in emphasis away from anultimate goal of fostering satisfaction in a mere passive expertise in 'ends' to one where we have at the heart of our process for both teacher and learner an active expertise in 'means'.

If conceptual development is to take place then schools must provide an environment where learning is seen as a creative process in which the students must take an active part. 'To make a concept his own, to truly comprehend it, a pupil has to take an active part in the process of its acquisition; sophisticated non-spontaneous concepts evolve with the aid of strenuous mental activity on the part of the child himself', as Vygotsky puts it.[10] Tasks should involve problem-solving and should be relevant to the needs and aspirations of each individual. Teaching must be tentative rather than authoritarian and the teacher must view the student as a whole person. The learning environment must have space for social interaction and also personal reflection. Within it structures like streaming have no place as they are anti-social and subject boundaries become an unnecessary constraint. Learning must be open-ended, individualized and determined by students and teachers in partnership. Teaching is seen as a dialogical activity where the teacher/pupil relationship is characterized by a mutual refining and defining of goals. That the teacher should, to use an American expression 'know where the student is coming from' is spelt out clearly by Vygotsky:

The investigator must understand the intrinsic bonds between the external tasks and the developmental dynamics and view concept formation as a junction of the adolescent's total social and cultural growth, which affects not only the contents but also the method of his thinking.[11]

Further implications for the role of the teacher can be found in this extract from one of the MACOS course teacher's guides: 'Our most intense pedagogical conviction is that over-simplification and dogmatism are the twin enemies of creative thought. Premature closure on a productive question can destroy imagination. Concepts are worthless unless they lead children to new explorations. Ideas, like facts, have a short life in memory if they are not assimilated by the child in his own way. The private world of children must be nurtured, not uprooted. Our task as teachers is to frame the problem clearly, which is often no more than asking the proper question'.

There isn't the need here to go into the reasons for adopting an integrated multidisciplinary approach to teaching and learning. From what has already been argued the reasons should really be self-evident. It is, however, worth pointing out that the holistic view of knowledge which underlies the whole integrated approach has clear implications for the teacher and the learner. Unlike the single subject, there are no artificial boundaries built up. It is the total vision which we call knowledge.

What then are the implications of those views for an effective assessment procedure of students' work? Stenhouse suggests

The process model is essentially a critical model not a marking model. It can never be *directed* towards an examination *as an objective* without loss of quality, since the standards of the examination then override the standards imminent in the subject.[12]

Do we in fact throw our process theory to the wind and resort to the tried and trusted testing methods? Even in our seemingly innovative teacher-controlled, teacher-assessed courses, are we forced to over-emphasize and rely in the end on the testing of recall of information? When it comes to the crunch are we in our assessment strategies in integrated humanities bound to be no different from those of the more conventional single-subject? In short, the solution seems to be to make the assessment procedure an integral part of the whole process. It should not be an impossible task and it is surely fundamental to genuine integrated humanities teaching and learning. We are concerned with testing skills and not the regurgitation of a wide range of factual knowledge and information. It may be desirable to emphasize particular skills in certain assignments — a task, like a project, involving detailed investigation and analysis might be marked for those skills, whereas a piece of work drawing together complex arguments on an issue might be assessed predominantly by how well these arguments can be put across in a discussion. We encourage enquiry and individualized work — it would be wrong to circumscribe the possibilities by the requirements of assessment.

The view of learning we have outlined stands in direct contrast with that normally held in schools. Concept and skills-based learning implies that:

1 The control of the learning process is held jointly within the relationship of student and teacher.
2 The learning process can best function where the social constraints of streaming and the intellectual constraints of subject boundaries are removed.
3 Motivation should be intrinsic and based on the perceived worth of an activity.
4 Cooperation rather than competitiveness is the order of the day.
5 Individuality and self-expression are highly valued within a cooperative social framework.

In conclusion, it must be seen that it is the view of knowledge, the view of teacher and learner and of the process of education described here that sets the integrated humanities approach apart. Critics might argue that what differentiates it is that it lacks the organization and structure that the more conventional single-subject approach upholds and which enables effective learning to take place. But it depends on how you define 'effective learning'. There clearly is an organization and structure to integrated humanities but not built on narrowly defined course content nor on an inert view of learning where comprehension is merely the unquestioning acquisition and manipulation of other people's ideas. Learning is an active, creative personalized and social process, where the role of the teacher is to facilitate and guide and where the students have responsibility for their own learning. It implies flexibility of curriculum and timetabling; it implies relationships based on mutual respect; it implies a democratic institution; it implies rigorous and continuous planning and, of course, a great deal of hard work. It also implies intrinsic rewards for the teacher who is prepared to get off his pedestal and join the essential humanity of the classroom.

Notes

1 BRUNER, J (1966) *Towards a Theory of Instruction*, Cambridge, MA, Bel Knap
2 BRUNER, J (1973) *The Relevance of Education*, New York, Norton
3 VYGOTSKY, L S (1962) *Language and Thought*, Cambridge, MA, MIT Press
4 STENHOUSE, L (1975) 'The process model' in *An Introduction to Curriculum Research*, London, Heinemann
5 DEWEY, J (1975) in GOLBY, M, GREENWALD, J and WEST, R (Eds) *Curriculum Design*, London, Croom Helm/Open University Press
6 HOLLY, D (1973) *Beyond Curriculum*, London, Hart-Davis McGibbon
7 PRING, R (1978) in LAWTON, D, *Theory and Practice of Curriculum Studies*, London, Routledge
8 MOORE and LAWSON (1978) in LAWTON, D, *Theory and Practice of Curriculum Studies*, London, Routledge
9 STENHOUSE, L (1975) *op cit*
10 VYGOTSKY, L S (1962) *op cit*
11 *Ibid*
12 STENHOUSE, L (1975) *op cit*

Oral History in Integrated Humanities

Carol Saunders

Oral history helps to create a more authentic and realistic view of the past. It draws upon the memories of people who have been largely ignored in history books. So, working class people, ethnic minorities, young people and women of all classes can be given a voice and so help the historian to reconstruct a more accurate historical record.

People have often found history to be dry and uninviting. Most traditional history books and lessons have been largely concerned with the ruling class, their lives, lifestyles and attitudes — a world which is outside most peoples' experience. Oral history can play an important role in making history come alive for the majority of people. New areas are opened up. Historians are now using oral history and researching the family, childhood and many aspects of people's daily lives. This approach is both more accessible and more interesting to most people. It can give people a sense of their own historical significance. It can make them feel that their own experiences are indeed valid pictures of the past and that their own views are true recollections of what happened. It can therefore help the less privileged, and especially the old, to develop a sense of self-respect and confidence as they see that they do have a specific place in history and a contribution to make to the writing of it. Oral history, then, is of mutual benefit to both the historian and the majority of people.

If it is agreed that history has tended to be concerned with lives and events outside most people's experience then must be a recipe for disaster as a subject in school if we believe that students become involved in learning when the subject matter is relevant to their own lives. Oral history can help to break down these barriers by providing an effective way of linking the students' own world with a wider past, so that the past and present can have some real meaning. So, students can be involved in finding out about the history of education by talking to a grandparent about their memories of their schooldays prior to 1944. They can then interview a parent or a neighbour who took the 11+ and so learn something about the tripartite system of education. Since so many of our students have parents who came to Britain in the 1950s, they may like to find out about their experiences on the journey, what they hoped to find in Britain, how they settled in once they arrived and then what they did actually experience when they had been living here a while. As a result of their oral history project students will realize that it is not only the powerful, privileged few who have a past, but that they, their families and their friends all have a place in history. So the subject begins to make more sense to them.

The Experiences Involved

Most students can talk. They can usually do so more fluently than they can write. They will also invariably have a friend or relative somewhere who enjoys telling them stories about things that have happened to them. This is the essence of oral history. Therefore this project is clearly accessible to *all* students regardless of age or academic ability, although younger and less academically motivated students may need greater help in planning their questions coherently and the projects will be taken to different levels. But the important point must be that students feel that they are able to get involved without in any way feeling intimidated by it.

A further consequence is that the relationship between the teacher and student of necessity changes. The teacher can no longer be the all-knowing disseminator of information. S/he becomes a facilitator, helping the students to consider their topic, organize their questions, look at possible interviewees and draw conclusions from their findings. The teacher may define the structure of the project but the students decide on the content. For it is they who are going to choose their interviewee and conduct the interview and therefore the bulk of the project is their own personal achievement. This will naturally encourage the teacher and student to develop a closer, less hierarchical relationship. The teacher's 'expertise' in interpreting evidence and in knowledge of existing sources for background reading, for example, may be useful to the student, but the teacher is also dependent on the support of the student to collect the evidence which is previously unknown to the teacher.

Oral history also encourages a closer relationship between the student and the interviewee. It stimulates empathy through identification with the life of others in the locality. It can bring together people from different age groups, racial backgrounds or social class, who would otherwise rarely meet. This must lead the students to a greater understanding of someone from a background different from their own and encourage them to be more understanding, tolerant and broad-minded.

The less privileged can benefit too. As interviewees, they also develop a contact and an understanding with someone with a life experience very different from their own. Since these groups in our society, particularly the old, are often lonely, they are likely to welcome their visitor and enjoy having the opportunity to sit and chat to someone who wants to hear stories about things that have happened to them. As their anecdotes are given validity, so the older person's self-respect and dignity can grow.

A closer relationship between the school and the local community develops. Through oral history, parents, grandparents, neighbours and other people in the area can all make a valuable contribution to the school. They, in turn, will see the school in a more positive light through the personal contact who has spent some time talking and listening to them.

The Skills Involved

During the course of an oral history project several types of skills may be developed. Firstly, it can provide assistance in the development of communication skills in both the spoken and the written word. While it is true that most students can talk, oral history makes them think about speaking clearly. Old people often have hearing difficulties and may even need to lip read. Thus the student will be forced not to mumble. Listening to the tape recording of their own voice will also make them think about speaking clearly.

Oral history puts the student into a listening role. Listening skills are very important yet many of our students don't seem to acquire them! Their interviewee might have a lot to say and the student must sit quietly, nodding encouragingly. On the other hand, the older person might be shy and embarrassed about being interviewed, particularly as it may be the first time they have used a microphone or heard their voice on tape. In this situation the student must encourage them to talk but without dominating the conversation themselves. All of this de-mands serious concentration.

Students develop an understanding of the difference between 'open' and 'closed' questions. As they prepare themselves before the interview they can discuss together the best wording of their questions.

They will develop the understanding that their job is to encourage the interviewee to talk as much as possible and therefore questions which result in 'yes' and 'no' answers are clearly unsuitable. They will learn to use questions which begin with 'who', 'what', 'where', 'why' and 'how' to get the person to talk fully.

Transcribing the tape into a coherent piece of writing is important if you, the teacher, want to develop certain writing skills. It is an intricate task listening to a tape and writing up the information into a readable piece of work. On the other hand you might want your students to write up just a part of their tape, selecting appropriate material. The beauty of this project is that very little writing has to be done, for the emphasis is on oral work. But if you want the students to be involved in writing there are plenty of possibilities.

Secondly, students develop an understanding of evidence as they look at and assess the material that they have been involved in collecting. This will mean that they have got to consider the reliability of their information. So if they have been talking to a miner about his experiences in 1926, it would not be surprising if he responded negatively towards the TUC. The student then learns that everyone has a personal point of view, a political perspective and therefore that all evidence contains bias. But through oral history they learn about this in a creative and personal way. They can then learn to evaluate, interpret and construct arguments from this evidence which they have collected from a living person.

Once pupils have developed an interest in interviewing someone they will want to find out more about their area of investigation. A third set of skills are then developed — those of enquiry. This can encourage them to use other sources. It can lead them into searches of the school or local library for books. It might even lead to browsing through old newspapers or magazines that someone has collected or looking at them in a reference library. This happened to a number of 14-year-olds in my class who were interviewing their grandparents about life in Leicester during the Second World War. They were quite prepared to pour over musty old newspapers in the library to find out more about their grandparents' experience. Some not only used the library for the first time but found out where it was located in the city. So, oral history involved them in learning techniques like using book indexes and the library cataloguing system as well as the experience of using the documents themselves. It is an excellent stimulant for arousing students' interest in a topic and encouraging them to develop enquiry skills.

The fourth set of skills encountered whilst doing an oral history project are technical ones. These are developed as the student becomes adept with the tape recorder and microphone. They will soon become familiar with the machinery. It is important that they have handled it before the interview and are confident of using it as they are likely to be required to make their interviewee feel comfortable when speaking into a microphone. Once they have completed their interview they might even edit extracts from the recording by using two tape recorders to improve the quality of the final tape.

A number of social skills are developed as students go out into the local community and are involved in forming relationships with people that they would not normally spend much time with. This will assist them in developing tact, patience and the ability to communicate and listen to others.

Oral history will also help young people to understand someone else's life. By being with someone older or someone from a different culture or class background they can hear a personal account of experiences differ. This may not only lead the students to develop understanding of what it is like to be someone else and how people's experiences differ. This may lead the students to not only develop empathetic skills but also encourage them to become more understanding, tolerant and broadminded towards different people. It can also help them to understand, as they put themselves into someone else's shoes, why people have conflicting views and attitudes.

Oral history encourages cooperation. This sort of project does not naturally lend itself to a competitive and individualistic approach. Not only do teachers and students develop a more equal relationship but so too do groups of students. They can work together planning their questions and practise them on each other before they go off to perform the real interview. They might also learn to use the tape recorder as a group, or a number of students, who might already be familiar with the equipment, can teach other students the technique. When the interview is completed they can listen to teach other's tapes and so evaluate the evidence together. Learning to work cooperatively is an important skill, yet it is too often competition which is tolerated and even encouraged in the classroom. It is also worth noting that it is not always the academic student who produces a good interview tape. Very often they are made by the students who are usually less motivated at school but who are good talkers and who are often related to, or friendly with people who have the most interesting memories. These recollections can be shared with the rest of the group and so the less academic student is for once given a chance to feel a sense of achievement in school.

The Context of Oral History Teaching

Oral history can be used in many different contexts within integrated humanities. It might be useful to have a personalized account from someone who has lived for many years in the neighbouring area if students are studying continuity and change in the local community. It could be used when students are doing work on the family. They might be involved in family history projects in which they are collecting old photographs, letters, documents, newspaper cuttings, memories and mementos. They could add an interview with a grandparent or parent about their childhood memories or their schooldays. This would encourage the family to become more involved with the student's work and also would help the student to see whether their parent(s) felt similarly about their schooldays to the way they feel themselves. One 14-year-old lad who interviewed his father about his school life in the forties declared that he would never again be rude about 'the old days': interviewing his father brought the tripartite system alive to this student and so helped him to understand what it would be like to have your educational future decided upon one day at the age of 11.

People can be interviewed on a variety of topics such as their work, their experiences in relation to war, housing, entertainment, holidays and leisure activities, health care, unemployment or transport. This may be as part of a project concerned with that particular topic, or it could simply be done as a piece of work in its own right. Whatever the context, oral history interviews will encourage students to see that learning from people is a valuable experience and that their family, friends and neighbours all have valid recollections of the past.

Setting up an Oral History Project

Choosing an Interviewee

The first thing students need to consider is who might be an appropriate person for them to interview. Their choice will depend upon the nature of the project that has been set. If the aim of the work is simply to allow students to pursue an individual piece of research in which they should include an interview, then they have the freedom to choose from a wide range of people. But if the context is that of, say, education prior to comprehensivization, then students are limited to people that they know who have been educated in a grammar or secondary modern school. If they were asked to do a project on changes in their local community, they would be well advised to choose someone elderly who had lived through many alterations in the neighbourhood.

It is worth pointing out to students that they should consider the age the interviewee would have been at the time they are interested in investigating. If, for instance, they were researching about life during the thirties then it would be foolish to interview a granny who was only 7 at the time because her memories would be a child's view of the world and inappropriate for discovering about those times in general. If, however, the student was required to do some research on childhood games in the thirties then this interviewee *would* be appropriate. Similarly, if the student was finding out about fashions in the sixties her 65-year-old grandfather would not be the best person to talk to. Instead she would be well advised to interview her 40-year-old mother who would have been between 15–25 and therefore interested in this issue at that time.

The table below might be useful to students:

TABLE 1:   To establish the age of people at various points in this century

Birth date	Age in: 1900	1910	1920	1930	1940	1950	1960	1970	1980
1880	20	30	40	50	60	70	80	90	100
1890	10	20	30	40	50	60	70	80	90
1900		10	20	30	40	50	60	70	80
1910			10	20	30	40	50	60	70
1920				10	20	30	40	50	60
1930					10	20	30	40	50
1940						10	20	30	40
1950							10	20	30
1960								10	20
1970									10

It is possible that some students might have difficulty finding someone to interview — perhaps their friends or family are not willing to participate, or the student does not know anyone with appropriate experience. Old people's homes are ideal resources to tap in this situation. Many of the older people would be only too pleased to help out and be given a chance to chat about the 'old times' to an eager youngster. Some students feel embarrassed about their families for a variety of reasons, and feel that their parents have not got anything interesting or relevant to say. In this situation they should be encouraged to proceed with the interview nevertheless and thus discover that everyone has a valid view of the past.

Whoever is chosen should be contacted with a suggested date for the interview and an explanation of the project. How the student contacts the interviewee will very much depend upon the relationship. If it is someone they do not know very well, then a brief letter explaining who they are and the purpose of them writing would be most appropriate. If it is someone they have never met before such as an old person in an old people's home then it would be wise for the student to visit them in advance so that student and interviewee are familiar with one another when the final interview takes place.

Background Research

Before the students go out into the community to conduct the interview they need to find out some information about the area that they are investigating. This is important because students will not be able to ask informed questions without prior knowledge of their topic. So, if someone was interested in interviewing their grandmother about her experiences in the Second World War, they would need to find out about what life was like in Britain at that time. Details about black-outs, air-raid shelters, rationing, bombing and gas masks would be appropriate background research. But they would not in this context need to look into the various campaigns of the war, since these did not directly involve the student's grandmother. A book such as Fiona Reynoldson's *War At Home*,[1] would be a useful resource for such background research. The student might, however, have a relative who was involved in the war as a soldier. If she or he wished to interview this person about their wartime experience then it would be appropriate to research certain campaigns which were most closely connected with the interviewee's role in the war. It would not be necessary or useful to research in detail the whole of the war.

Another student might know an interesting old lady who likes to talk about 'the old days'. She should investigate a broad range of topics that the woman might have experienced — like education, transport, work, housing and clothes at the beginning of the twentieth century. Her project would cover a number of aspects of life at the turn of the century. *The History of the Modern World*[2] series on themes like 'The twenties' or 'The turn of the century' are useful books for 11 to 15-year-olds. So too are the *Into the Past*[3] series. These are short, simple books written around contemporary photographs and cover topics like 'Entertainment in 1900' and 'In the street in 1900' and 'At work in the 1930s'.

Once the student has found out some useful information about the topic it can be written up as an introduction to the interview to set the context. This can be as long or as short as you want it to be. It is important to bear in mind that the aim of this project is to emphasize the importance of oral and not written work.

The Questions

The aim of the interview is to draw out as much information as possible from the interviewee. To do this students will need to write a questionnaire as they will not remember all the things they want to find out about. Whilst they are doing this they will need close guidance.

Firstly, it is important that their list of questions should be given some logical shape. The questions should flow smoothly from one to the other. This will help the interviewee to feel more comfortable, as though being guided through the interview, and that the student knows what she is doing. If it is not planned adequately and questions are fired at the interviewee in a haphazard way, then the response will be hesitant and awkward with a lot of repetition. It also makes it easier later on when the student is expecting to transcribe or analyze the interview. So, if the student is interviewing her mother about 'Life in the fifties', then it should be carefully constructed into a series of topics starting with, perhaps, family life, then going on to schooling, leisure and entertainment, work and so on.

The questionnnaire should begin with simple specific questions written in familiar language. These should then lead on to questions which are more searching. This will help to make the interviewee feel at ease and confident that s/he can answer the questions. It also helps to give the logical shape required. If the student is interviewing a grandparent on schooldays, s/he might start with a question like 'How old were you when you first went to school?' and 'What type of school was it?' Such questions can then lead on to others expecting more detailed responses like 'What were the classrooms like?', 'What diffe-rent lessons did you have?', 'What were the teachers like?' and so on. Questions should never be too complex or involve more than one issue, or else only part of the question will be answered and the interviewee will probably be too confused to answer *that* very well.

Students will also need to consider which sort of questions will give the required detailed response. They will therefore need to understand that 'Did you all sit in rows?' will receive a much shorter answer than 'How was your classroom laid out?' To understand the difference between 'open' and 'closed' questions is not an easy task but it is important if the student is to conduct a successful interview. I have found the best way to teach this is to get them to do practice interviews on each other. I get them to sit in pairs and ask a partner questions on either memories of primary school or childhood games. Each is asked to jot down at least ten questions in which as much as possible has to be found out about the partner's experience of the given topic. They soon learn that if they start their questions with 'why', 'what', 'how', they are more likely to receive the sort of answers they want.

Using a Tape Recorder

Students will need to be familiar with the tape recorder and microphone if they are going to use them at the interview. It is advisable that they should be used, otherwise large chunks may be omitted, as the interviewer won't have time to write down everything or else, if the student *does* attempt to write down all that is said, the interview will become slow and tedious, for both parties, as the interviewer scribbles away furiously.

Most schools these days have a number of cassette tape recorders. While they might not be of the best quality they do at least enable all students to have access to one. If it is possible, the student should use a tape recorder with a separate microphone since the built-in microphone type tend to pick up a constant background hum which can seriously reduce the quality of the recording.

Students will need to buy a cassette tape if they wish to keep the recording and many of them certainly will. It is always worthwhile for a humanities department to have a number of blank tapes available for those students who are not able to bring their own.

Learning to use the tape recorder can be done at the same time as the students do their practice interview with a partner in school. This helps them gain confidence using the machinery and to become familiar with the sound of their voices on tape. They will quickly become adept at handling the equipment.

Students should be reminded that the aim of the interview is to collect as much information from the interviewee as possible. Therefore their input should be kept to a minimum. Instead of speaking in agreement, the student should nod encouragingly. They certainly should not venture to disagree or interrupt. If the interviewee wanders off the subject this should be allowed to continue until there is an appropriate moment for the subject to be reintroduced.

The Interview Itself

The students should have their fully prepared questionnaires with them and perhaps a number of articles that might trigger off recollections by the interviewees. These may include things like old photographs, newspaper cuttings and odd items like a gas mask or old ornament.

It is best if the interview can take place at the informant's house. It must be a place where the interviewee can feel at ease and confident talking about old personal memories. So school would *not* be an ideal environment. The interviewee might also have various mementos at home which might be shown to the student, so enriching the experience. It is also a valuable opportunity for a student to go into someone else's home and imagine what it would be like to live there and be that person.

It is preferable if the two can be alone. If other members of the family are involved then they might disagree on details of events and end up quarrelling on the tape! I have known students to be interviewing their grandmothers with their grandfathers interrupting every so often with the 'correct' version of the story! Others have experienced their interviewee being dominated on tape by another member of the family if the interviewee was slightly unsure of herself or the other person was a more dominant character. Sometimes, however, the presence of a second party can be positive in that one person can stimulate the memory of another and the tape be correspondingly enriched. But it's a risky business!

If the student is not well known to the interviewee then a pre-visit is advisable. The student should be careful not to get too involved in discussing anything on their questionnaire at this stage because it is often difficult to do a repeat performance. The object of the pre-visit should be merely to get to know each other and feel at ease in each other's company. On arrival the student should chat to the interviewee to make him or her feel comfortable. It will also be helpful to show the interviewee the tape recorder and the microphone. The student should also look out for any loud background noises that might interfere with the quality of the tape. If a loudly ticking clock can be moved out of the room without making the interviewee feel anxious, then it should be done at the beginning, before the interview takes place. Once all these preparations are completed the student is ready to proceed.

Carol Saunders

Transcribing the Interview

While writing out the interview is not a necessary part of an oral history project, for many students it is a valuable aspect. Many students feel proud of their own personal piece of oral research and are quite prepared to transfer the interview onto paper. For non-academic students this is a rare opportunity to feel confident about writing. They feel involved with the project largely because the information comes from someone they know and like, rather than an anonymous book. They understand clearly what they are doing as they have devised the project themselves. This is an excellent chance for these students to practice their English writing skills — particularly their punctuation.

There may be other students who prefer to write just the important aspects of the tape out. This is also a useful task since they are weighing up all the evidence and selecting only that which is relevant — a very important skill.

Analysis

When students return to the classroom with their tapes and/or transcriptions they always love to listen to each other's tapes or read the interviews. This is an important part of the oral history project which should be encouraged and given time since it further encourages students to work cooperatively and gives status to the work they have done — and therefore to themselves.

They can discuss the evidence they have personally collected with their friends, and listen to the experiences that the others had. They can also write about what they have learnt from the material they now have. They should point out any problems they came across and consider how they might improve the project — by adding an interview of someone with a different perspective, perhaps. It is also useful to encourage the students to think more generally about the use to the historian of oral sources.

Summary

All young people should encounter the experience of oral history. It is important that they realize that they, their friends and family all have valid recollections of the past and can locate themselves in history.

Oral history, too, readily lends itself to an integrated approach between different subject areas. There can be few projects that can boast such a wide range of skills and experiences. While many may be encountered in other humanities subjects like social studies, geography and English language, here they are all located in just one piece of work.

Finally, oral history is accessible to *all* students. Whatever their age or academic ability they are able to get involved in this type of project without being intimidated by it. All students can talk and some of the poorest academic achievers talk the best. This gives these students an opportunity to display their skills.

Since all young people should be exposed to the experience and all of them can achieve success with such a project then one should clearly form part of the core curriculum. It is ideally suited to mixed ability teaching since it is accessible to all and encourages cooperation between students of different levels of ability. Integrated humanities, with its flexible timetable would seem the most appropriate place for it.

Notes

1 REYNOLDSON, F (1980) *War at Home*, London, Heinemann Educational.
2 *The History of the Modern World Series*, (1973), London MacDonald Educational.
3 *Into the Past Series*, (1981) London, Longmans.

Integrated Humanities in the Inner City School

G. A. Coleby

I had been working in the county of Leicestershire for about a decade sampling and hopefully contributing to forward-looking educational practice in the humanities area. But deep down I was a city person and working in the county was a bit like being at university — pleasant but unreal for me. I was brought up in London and ILEA-educated, and opted to live in the city of Leicester when I worked in the county. Whether I liked all aspects of living in the city was irrelevant. My intellectual affinity was with the Leicestershire Plan (city education used to be separate and very different) but my heart was in the city.

So, somehow I had to escape to the city. But that was easier wished than done. In two years of looking, not one job in the humanities came up that I could go for. The main reasons for this are nationwide: overstaffing, contraction, falling rolls, amalgamation, etc. But there was also a city problem of not really recognizing the importance of integrated humanities and an almost sole reliance on separate humanities subjects. I just had to bide my time and wait and wait...

And then it happened. A phone call late one night. A school in Leicester needed a few extra teachers for one year only to assist with developments. Are you interested? Before the last word was uttered over the phone I was packed and ready. My briefcase was in tip-top condition for a 'radical' teacher: dustless chalk (but only one stick), some recently produced resources and a few carefully polished and rehearsed John Holt phrases. Things were moving. The next day I had an informal interview with the Principal.

I got the job. I was to start next term. I was one of six extra teachers needed to cope with the school's fast changing situation. From what I could gather the 'new' community college was currently working on three sites: the new building, only half complete, the old boy's school and the old girl's school. The challenge the new Principal had was to develop a single entity out of two amalgamated single sex schools in the inner city with a large multi ethnic catchment area.

Still, I wanted to work in the city and be a part of this development so I accepted the secondment for a year. (Don't most normal people get seconded to universities or polys?) I knew it would be different from my previous experiences but knowing does not always lessen the impact. In that briefcase I also had a few other things: my educational perspectives, prejudices, principles and experiences. These were to be exposed to a new group of people and I did not know how they would be received . . . My abstract thoughts were then disturbed by another contact with the Principal: would I take on another role apart from that as an 'experienced teacher'? The Head of Resources was to take on a new role and there was no-one to fill it. I accepted and this, at least, made my anxieties more concrete. Even though I had always had an active interest in resource-based learning and organizing learning materials this was a big step. And the staff knew I was from the county and I was one of the 'Principal's men'. What strategy should I adopt to bring about some form of significant development in the one year? If it were a permanent post I could walk around carefully on egg-shells but it wasn't and I'm not very good at that anyway, but I'd have to at least try to understand current practices and procedures. My understanding, however, was bound to be affected by heresay about the new school. 'It was a tough school'. 'It was full of bitterness due to the outcome of amalgamation'. 'It had secondary modern staff'. 'It's not the kids but the staff that you'll have to watch out for'. 'Don't do it!' Experience, reading and interest had shown me that institutions had a powerful effect on individuals and this seemed to be the case at this place. In the city, before reorganization, there were real grammar schools and 'others'. The 'others' had various titles but in reality they were secondary moderns. Being a secondary modern teacher seemed to lead to a lowering of self-esteem and in many schools seemed to result in either an apeing of grammar school styles 'to prove them wrong' or to adopt a siege mentality 'we are dealing with failures; we cannot succeed'. The 'new' school seemed to bear this out and the staff, with a significant number of non-graduates, did seem less willing to put large-scale educational views forward and status was far more jealously guarded than in my previous experience. Even more open staff suffered from the atmosphere of the old 'city': an unwillingness to see education beyond the walls of the school and having a minimal contact with other schools regarding educational cooperation. To me this all resulted in often very able teachers not fulfilling their potential and appearing cynical and prematurely middle-aged. The organization of the city and the old school seemed more mysterious and closed and career structures poorly defined or even non-existent.

After being there for only a short time my view changed. 'Secmoditis' existed but not in as extreme a form as thought likely. Many of those most unhappy after amalgamation had left, others had been promoted and enhanced and there seemed to be no organized opposition to change. So what was I to do? I had no desire to be a technical type of resources teacher, where I would simply respond to other teachers' 'needs' nor did I want a swish model of progressive resource-based learning, which few of our teachers could use. So, I had to try to develop a Centre which would grow as the curriculum grew. But this meant that I had a role in curriculum development that was neither official nor housed in one particular department. Revolution by consent? This was the time to develop my diplomatic skills.

Teaching not far off a full timetable, setting up a new resources centre in a new building while working on a split-site situation and wanting to change the educational world called for some pretty stiff prioritization if I was not to go under fast. My teaching had to be at least adequate: who likes a curriculum innovator who cannot teach? Though I had bigger goals than my own teaching, it would be one way to provide a model for future growth.

As the first few weeks passed it began to dawn on me that the whole curriculum needed reviewing and pushing, for this was going to have to be a main priority. Soon, the staff as a whole came to the conclusion that this was the case and a review body was set up — more of that later. To gain credibility I had to make an impact in the Centre itself: my official responsibility. But here I underestimated the task. It was not just a case of getting a reprographic unit working, audio-visual systems worked out and developing a library, but getting the staff to see them as a whole unit to assist in classroom learning. And I had no experience!

However, being in the Centre gave me at least one big advantage over almost everyone else in the school: I saw the materials that teachers were using and from that could develop further understanding as to the real nature of the curriculum. Apart from the few teachers who survived by personal charm and the phantoms of the banda, I began to build a picture of the curriculum. It was here that I discovered the real barriers to curriculum development: galloping isolation. Most teachers' experience of teaching was as an isolated and isolating experience, not from the pupils but from their colleagues. Most teachers were resourcing their lessons with almost solely own-produced worksheets. Now, of course, some were very good, but these were rarely shared and others were very poor but seldom seen by their colleagues. This situation had all the disadvantages of highly individualized teaching and none of the advantages. But for a change to take place we had to change the structure of the curriculum to create space for teachers to be able to work more effectively. No longer should staff use the offset as a super banda churning out well-produced tat and no longer should education be seen as the deliberate measuring out of daily doses of worksheets. There was more to education. But how could the staff be persuaded of this? At least, in the current practices the pitfalls were known. What about the future?

Luckily, the necessity for change both within school and in education as a whole was accepted by most. So getting the issue on the agenda was not difficult. In a way the school as a whole suffered from the same problem in general as the major departments did in particular and what follows is an account of how curriculum has developed in many schools in Britain and the problems it has caused.

I produced the following staff briefing paper which summarizes the way forward for the school's curriculum as I saw it:

The need for a flexible curriculum — the dangers of compromise

What a child brings to education: A child brings emotions, culture, class, language, gender and experience to school. This affects how they feel and act.

In school a curriculum is imposed on them: Usually at secondary level this is in a traditional form and is based on learning subjects. Curriculum development has been seen as the continual adding of subjects as the pressure arose. Apart from the 'basics' which seem unchallenged for their place on the curriculum, for example, maths, English, RE, many other areas have pushed for their share and many schools boast openly of the dozens of subjects that their pupils have the chance of studying.

Outside pressures grow: The child's outside world is also pushing for a place in his or her mind. The family, the community, friends, the mass media, the world of work, the government, MSC, TVEI and YTS — all are trying to justify and develop their right to time.

G. A. Coleby

The traditional response: The traditional response to change by teachers was simple: you simply add on more subjects to the curriculum as needs arose. But this process has gone as far as logic will take it. We now have an *OVERCROWDED* curriculum, which can take no more. And here teachers start to feel threatened. What does this overcrowding lead to?

(i) *Fragmentation*: As more subjects are put in you get less time for each one. The teachers have less time to get to know individual needs. More classes lead to the teachers having to do more preparation, therefore doing it less well. Students end up with a diet of never-ending worksheets and a minimum of real first-hand learning.

   Teachers start to sink and have less time to work with others to be creative in their salvation. The cycle then repeats itself. . . .

   The effects on students can be catastrophic: 'The child may also react to uninteresting teaching by adults and may be upset by a confusing, impersonal and frequently unintegrated plan of departmentalized education.'[1]

   Recently, many reports on education have also cast doubts on the traditional curriculum coping. Hargreaves has shown that apart from the few who have switched off outwardly there is a whole army who have switched off *INWARDLY* and we should be more concerned with these for at least the former group have their spirit intact.

(ii) *Rigidity*: In a strange way the traditional pattern is very rigid. It appears not to be so but in practise thwarts most attempts to integrate life. It is a fairly static structure, which cannot cope with change without much pain and continual timetable revision. Where on the present curriculum can we teach about new technology, cultural diversity, unemployment, democracy, community involvement, world issues, leisure studies etc? These things cannot be 'added' on to the present structure or it will become even more fragmented. So usually we do not do them properly.

   The traditional curriculum also suffers from time-lags and syllabus addiction: 'We have not got time to drift off the subject. . . .'

A way forward: A way forward is to rethink the purpose of education. If education is to develop a society of bored, unthink-

80

ing, form-filling automatons, who are essentially passive, then we have come up with the ideal form of education. But if we wish to create thinking, sensitive, active, critical and positive young citizens then we need to change. The form of change is debateable but the necessity is not. We must not fall into the trap of rewriting the curriculum without rethinking the structure. We will never get the perfect curriculum: it will always change and develop as needs do, and most curriculum revisions fail if they concentrate on the content and not the process of education. We can, however, get the structure right. We can decide the kind of skills that students should have the opportunity of learning while at school.

The skills: These would include literacy, numeracy, social literacy, aesthetic awareness, technological skills, problem-solving skills, decision-making skills, performing skills, teamwork skills, communication skills, etc. The point is that these will not rest happily in 'subjects': they are multidisciplinary.

The structure: The structure has got to be flexible, to be able to cope with change without massive restructuring, to cope with in-service teacher education and training without disturbing the students too much. It has got to create time for teachers to meet and plan and discuss and evaluate and support each other. It has got to provide the security and comradeship that a subject-based education can no longer do.

I would suggest that the structure would be based on a core of areas that would cover the essential needs that students require. These areas themselves would be flexible and able to introduce new learning when appropriate and 'rest' other areas. These would also be block timetabled with other broad core areas so that potential cooperation could be developed. For example the core could be:

> English and communications
> Integrated humanities
> Integrated science
> Design
> Maths and numeracy

This would lead to at least five public examinations. Similarly, there would be two option blocks, which could consist of some traditional subjects or a number of modular based courses, for example, every student in the fourth and fifth year could have a ten-week computer course.

I recognize that not all of these more flexible approaches could be embarked on at once. Science could remain separate for a while as could design, but what must occur is that new curriculum can develop without further structural change. The important corollary is that all areas have the same time allocation and faculties themselves should timetable their own area. Hence a science team and a humanities team could agree to work together on a study of, say, ecology or pollution. There would be no compulsion to do so but it would be possible, as other combinations would be.

The big spin-off is for the staff, no longer working alone in little boxes where the best idea can fail, but working as a team together developing a real educational experience for the children. Not hemmed in by narrow and artificial barriers we can help demystify the world that we hope our students will improve; we will be able to have the flexibility to give all students that little extra special attention they all need; we will be able to bounce ideas and experiences off each other in a professional way, not in a snatched corridor situation.

Since that paper was written much discussion has taken place and the curriculum review body has accepted the basic idea of a five-core/two-option structure. The option columns are to be modularized and a new form of accreditation is to be negotiated with our examination board. But in a way this cannot be a conclusion but the end of one stage. The staff as a whole have to be convinced of the need to change not just in theoretical but in practical terms.

The next stage of the development must be to create a timetable structure that will allow this new skills-based curriculum to grow. No longer will we have the security of an externally set syllabus and cupboards full of known resources, so new security will have to be created. The way to do this is to put team planning and preparation on the timetable as number one priority. Being able to work together and share experiences will put back into education a vital missing ingredient: solidarity.

Note

1 Quoted from the Citizens Committee on Children of New York discussing children absent from school.

Patriarchy, Ethnocentrism and Integration

Carolyn Robson

We are after all trying to create an integrated society, and a great many of our pupils, whilst retaining their racial and religious 'peculiarities' think of themselves as British. I think that we need to be made fully aware of the differences, but I think in teaching we must be careful not to create divisions. Following this my history syllabus and the humanities syllabus developing, is and will remain basically British.

These are the words of a Head of Humanities Faculty quoted in 1973 by Townsend and Brittan in *Multiracial Education: Need and Innovation*, (Schools Council Working Paper 50).

Twelve years on and one wonders how typical this comment still is of educational thinking, both within the humanities and in schools at large, despite a decade of increasing awareness of the issues of racism, and, to some extent, sexism. Despite over sixty years of female suffrage in Britain and decades of rhetoric and active feminism, for instance, how much of the curriculum is still male-orientated in order not to 'create divisions', thus effectively maintaining the *status quo* of patriarchy?

To some degree all cultures are ethnocentric and patriarchal considering their own cultural values (albeit male ones) to be objective reality. It is only a short step from this state to the more sophisticated hierarchical categorizations, believing in superiority/inferiority, domination/subordination, that go to make up structural features in society, namely racism and sexism, through which the ideas and attitudes of ethnocentrism and patriarchy are constructed and sustained by the practices, procedures and institutions of society. Racism and sexism are thus not simply forms of prejudice but sophisticated forms of oppression, domination and power.

The effects of society's wider racism and sexism are always felt in schools in that they cannot exist in isolation. The education system is merely a part of British society and as such is faced with inequalities that exist, such as those caused by the extent and depth of institutionalized racism and sexism. Schooling is an integral part of the operations of institutionalized racism and sexism, so that debates about racism and sexism in the curriculum are often fundamental arguments about the nature of society. It is necessary to understand the nature of ideologies that support racism and sexism and not merely dismiss them as crazy or irrational. It is necessary to be aware of the images conveyed by media, by textbooks, and by the features of racism, for instance, entrenched in immigration and nationality legislation. Teachers, however, too frequently reject education's role in perpetuating racism or sexism, even if unintentionally. This perpetuation is partially caused by a 'non-fit' between the real world and the world inside school, created by the teaching profession's power to define what is valuable knowledge.

Education, like race or gender, is a moral, intellectual and political issue involving values, standards and judgments, and it must be acknowledged that an education system which teaches British history from a white man's viewpoint, and ignores the facts of colonialism, is a system in which racist ideology is institutionalized. An education system which ignores or patronizes the female role in history ignoring the elements of exploitation in our family system is institutionalizing sexism. Teachers are bound to operate within the framework of the economic, political, social and cultural realities of which the education system is only a part, but it is not a requirement of education to preserve a *status quo* of social inequality, otherwise it becomes merely an instrument of stability and control. In humanities education we are not and cannot be neutral (despite the attempts by the Humanities Curriculum Project, for instance, to present teacher neutrality as part of its rationale) for to remain 'neutral' is to condone the inequality of society rather than to challenge it. We are not compelled to fit children for pre-destined places in society as it is. We do not have to imply by our inaction that social patterns are inevitable. As Brent Education Committee puts it:

> The Council does not expect schools/teachers to be held accountable for racism in society. However they must and will be held responsible and accountable for the racism which is inherent in the education service itself and which in turn leads to the unquestioning acceptance of racism in society.[1]

Education should be about critical thinking, about confronting hostile attitudes and closed minds that degrade people, about challenging assumptions and attacking injustice. Yet much of the work in the humanities curriculum, traditionally the faculty area prescribed to tackle contentious political issues, has drawn upon unquestioned images of a male-dominated, eurocentred world. There has been stereotyping and tokenism of women and blacks, and a 'Third World' picture of disease, drought and death, with no explanation of the socio-economic or political background of exploitation that produces poverty and inequality. Geographers describe socio-economic and political differences through their maps: they do not, however, explain or challenge the underlying reasons for the spatially-expressed differences.

Since the later 1960s and Powell's 'rivers of blood' speech, the tightening immigration controls, and increasingly influential but complex philosophy and range of practices, often labelled 'multiculturalism', has developed in British educational thinking. Its recognition, through phases of assimilation, integration and cultural pluralism of the white role in perpetuating racism has moved away from the 'problems' of 'immigrant' children (that term itself being a misnomer) in schools, to the problems of institutional racism. The curriculum in some schools has moved towards reflecting and valuing the diversity of lifestyles, beliefs and cultural traditions that post-war immigration has brought to Britain. (This is not to say that *all* schools have developed along these lines, for many, particularly the predominantly 'white' schools, have remained firmly entrenched in 'assimilationist' thinking, similar to the views of the Head of Humanities quoted above.) This 'multiculticulturalism' has often been supported by disputed psychological evidence about self-concept in blacks, by real fears of worsening racial conflict and brutal authoritarian responses among the white majority. At one end of the political spectrum, 'multiculturalism' has been seen as radical, dangerous or irrelevant, just as 'women's studies' may have been so dismissed. They have both been perceived as 'political activism', controversial or even a 'time-bomb'. At the other extreme they have been seen as a sophisticated white racism, male chauvinism, a control mechanism using token gestures of liberalism and equality to disguise real discrimination.

And multiculturalism can, in fact, be seen as refusing to address questions of class and gender difference, power and control, and therefore smoothing out wrinkles in society whilst maintaining *status quo* patterns. Education's move into multiculturalism, accompanied by policy-making at all levels may have actually furthered the racist cause by diverting and pacifying. Words of harmony and tolerance, or equality, are frequent in policy statements from the DES, the LEAs and schools, but actions are poorly defined. There tends to be a moralistic evangelism, but ignorance or fear of active commitment to change. This problem exists whether the intentions of policies are unintentionally or deliberately vague, diversionary and pacifying.

One of the school responses to multiculturalism or to gender issues has been to insert discussion and celebration of cultural and gender difference into subjects such as history, geography and RE. In other words the humanities faculty has often been a suitable 'junk box' for contentious political issues and these issues have merely been seen in terms of curriculum slots, rather than concerns of the whole school in terms of the reappraisal of relationships, attitudes and aims. Integrated humanities courses may have gladly taken on board these issues, quite obviously central to the key understanding of human societies, but in many cases all that has been achieved is a marginalization and a packaging of the issues into separate slots, such as the 'persecution and prejudice' unit of the Joint Matriculation Board Integrated Humanities 'O' level course. Outside these slots integrated humanities has largely continued to teach about the dominant culture, ie, white and male, using heavily ethnocentric and patriarchal resources. Too frequently again, the humanities faculty has concentrated on cultural celebration, with many courses, especially those of lower or middle schools, demonstrating ignorance or avoidance of racism and sexism. Examples of this include use of the generic term 'man' to mean all people, or themes with titles such as 'Who are the British?' which solely cover the invasions of the Romans, Saxons, Vikings and Normans, with a dabbling into pre-history but little or no concentration on immigration in the nineteenth or twentieth centuries. In my experience, Leicestershire high school humanities courses, for instance, with all their enviable 'freedom' of content and methods have actually been rarely more than a scissors and paste rejiggling of traditional subjects, or a heavy reliance on packaged learning, such as the 'Man a Course of Study' units, which themselves need considerable review.

What is integrated humanities about, if not about humanity and society, about empathy, sensitivity, about issues and problems of the modern world, about challenge and participation in society? It should not be an amalgam of core traditional subject content areas but a unique core of human learning containing not just empirical social studies but also the affective arts and literature. It should be skills-based but needs useful content to hang on, and it is that content selection that has provoked most problems in terms of identifying the really useful content and the underlying concepts. However it is no use concentrating on content change if the whole education system needs changing so that anti-racist or anti-sexist education does not become an end in itself in terms of specific themes but is viewed as part of the means by which society moves towards greater equality and social justice. Integrated humanities must be clear about its perspective with sexism and racism tackled at the forefront of change rather than marginalized into neat topics. There will also be little credibility for anti-sexist, anti-racist ideas if the medium fails to match the method. Ways must be found to improve social relations in the classroom, breaking down hierarchies based on age, sex, race and class through collaborative learning.

If one attempts to analyze the specific failures of anti-racist, anti-sexist strategies within the humanities faculty, certain obvious points can be made. The 'Third World' has suffered from patronizing post-colonialism and its peoples have been seen as passive recipients, victims of natural disasters or even gun-crazy terrorists. Dawn Gill's CRC report on modern geography courses in 1983 indicated that 'O' level and CSE examination boards emphasized 'Third World' problems, such as population, 'primitive' agriculture, migration to cities, without associated explanation of the social processes or the political-economic environment which creates the problems. A 'Blue Peter' mentality exists, orientated to appeals for aid for the 'unfortunate' peoples of poor countries, and development is too often perceived of as following the western model.

David Selby has suggested that school geographers would do well to take Kidron and Segal's *State of the World Atlas*[2] and relate it to the geography curriculum, using maps such as 'bullets and blackboards' (ratio of teachers to soldiers) or 'women workers' (describing sex discrimination in jobs). So many new humanities books in geography or other areas continue to fail to describe the North's real economic relationship to the South in spite of the Brandt Report of 1980 and its call for an understanding of the 'global imperative' — a recognition of the interdependent nature of the contemporary world where the problems of any nation or group can only be seen and understood or remedied within a global context.

Within the lower/middle school humanities curriculum a best-selling geography text, while claiming balance and objectivity has passages like that quoted by D. Wright:

3.1: People and Cultivation in the Forest Zone of West Africa. This man (ie close-up photograph of a man's head — black and frowning) is one of the inhabitants of the forest areas. Accurately describe his features. Perhaps make a drawing, adding labels to indicate those features which are distinctive.[3]

The photo-bias of the same book is another problem, common to many other text books in the humanities. Not one of the forty-seven colour photographs of Australia shows a black person and the photographs of South African black people show them only in subservient or menial roles. Imaginative writing calls for an even greater stress on white, generally male, middle-class experience such as imagining owning one of the claims at the Kimberley diamond mines! One presumes that a text book like this is not deliberately racist or sexist, but it is nevertheless hopelessly stereotyping world reality into neat, eurocentric male patterns, and maintaining a best-seller status while so doing.

In many respects the problems we are facing in education with regard to racism and sexism may be partly due to our failure to recognize their existence as not just prejudice but institutional power-based features. It may be hard for those of us brought up in a racist, sexist society, especially to the extent we may benefit (at least if male) from the privileges of that society, to see racism and sexism clearly. We seem to ignore or accept the sheer invisibility of women and blacks in texts, photographs, images and the curriculum as Dale Spender has shown in the case of women.

Other common problems within the humanities framework include the anthropological tendency to label peoples as 'primitive', or the images of 'noble savages' and also the evolutionism, which tends to hold western civilization as the pinnacle of potential human development. Early integrated humanities packages, such as Bruner's *Man: A Course of Study*, have been accused of following this evolutionist approach from the patriarchal ethnocentric standpoint of western society. Another criticism of much of the social-science-based humanities has been the tendency for its emphasis on statistical, quantitative or empirical research techniques to displace empathy, a process which underlines the point that integrated humanities should include the arts and creative elements as much as history, geography, sociology, economics and other 'social' subjects.

With particular regard to patriarchy there is too often a lack of awareness of the female point of view, involving what Dale Spender calls 'invisibility', an ignoring of women's concerns. It is vital that in integrated humanities pupils learn to be aware of the discrepancy between what is often *presented* as reality and what is *experienced* as reality by approximately 50 per cent of the world's population. Blatant sexism and stereotyping ought to be pointed out, such as the stereotype of the typical woman as economically inactive, married and having two children whereas, even in Western society, this actually applies to 5 per cent, making 95 per cent of women 'untypical'! Neither ought women to be shown as being *actually* often passive or ornamental, under-represented in terms of having access to decision-making, status and power, without direct comment on the subordination and oppression that this, in fact, involves. Population growth in the 'Third World' ought no longer be described in terms of 'women having too many children', nor ought a relatively new geography text book to contain six photographs of women pushing prams — an observation made by R. Beddis.[5]

Integrated humanities needs concern itself also about possible gender bias not just in terms of resources and topic areas, but also in terms of its possible image as 'female', where technology and sciences are perceived as 'male'. This may particularly influence option choices and career-motivated exam choices. Yet studying the human condition is surely no more 'female' than 'male' and an essential part of all education. In fact, of course, in terms of leadership positions humanities faculties are as male-oriented as any others! In classroom management also the two sexes need equal treatment by teachers, in terms of expectation and type of praise. Where individual learning programmes are proceeding with student directed assignments it is surely an important teacher role to take into account sexist stereotypes of areas of choice so that all students may pursue interests and careers that suit them as *individuals*, not as gender representatives.

These may reflect some of the problems or failures of humanities in confronting and challenging patriarchy and ethnocentrism, but there are ways forward and there have been plenty of individual successes. The fears and concerns of teachers when tackling contentious issues without the cloak of 'neutrality', for instance, have often been allayed by the team approach of integrated humanities, which can build up confidence and promote equal sharing in the racism/sexism awareness programmes necessary for staff themselves. This 'team sharing', so essentially part of integrated humanities organization, can help orientate staff in their individual perceptions, reassessment and redefinitions of reality and their distancing from a racist, sexist society. It can also importantly aid the development of an analytical framework for action, such as observing and then acting on ethnic/sexist jokes, stereotypes, abuse, bias. Finally the team can move on into protests and public statements, including criticisms of published material and exam board criteria and content. The staff can learn as a team how to 'take the lid off things' and generate the right atmosphere for free discussion without retreating into a false neutrality and, whilst although feeling recoil and horror at attitudes and prejudices prevalent in students, be able to support one another in reacting strongly but not emotionally, working on logical contradictions such as 'they take all our jobs' and 'they're all on the dole'.

An essential part of anti-racism or anti-sexism in schools is direct awareness programmes in the curriculum. These have often been most effective if starting with a historical or distancing process which may allow discussion to proceed without interference from strong emotional reactions. Relating to racism, these historical or distancing techniques might include studies of the Holocaust or apartheid in South Africa or, relating to sexism, might include suffragettes. However, the crucial test of this approach is its effectiveness as an anti-racist or anti-sexist teaching strategy when confronting present-day realities. C. Mulhern pointed out in an ALTARF published in 1978 that 'it can be perplexing to find pupils soundly condemning the African homelands system, while at the same time arguing that "we should send our blacks home"'.

Another interesting and challenging method of tackling racism and sexism is through experiential learning, especially simulations, games and drama exercises. Groby Commnity College's 'purple armbands' experiment, documented in the BBC publication *Multi cultural Education*[6] and filmed in *Anglo-Saxon Attitudes* (BBC film in the *Multi Cultural Education* series) was one such experience. Games such as *Rafa Rafa* and *Star Power* (available through Christian Aid) are similarly useful exercises on cultural awareness and power structures. The UNESCO units 3.1[7] provide other imaginative and effective experiences, and Katz's exercises in *White Awareness: Handbook for Anti-Racism Training*, provide excellent ideas for staff and student awareness programmes, in particular the exercises *Designing a Racist Community* and *Circle Break In*.

A third method of awareness raising is to tackle directly modern racism or sexism by reviewing society as it is. This method can be the most difficult to tackle since it may provoke the most antagonism and prejudice. It may be advisable to seek 'expert' help from outside the school environment like the Mobile Education Unit run by Leicestershire County Council or various mobile theatre groups who may provide greater knowledge, experience and a necessary distance which may help counteract the hostility and ignorance of students. Films such as *The Eye of the Storm* (USA, 1973, Concord Films), *The Life and Death of Steve Biko* (Granada TV, 1976) and *Racism the 4th R* (ALTARF, BBC 2 Open Door) are also extremely thought-provoking and effective. Other useful anti-racist exercises focus on immigration and nationality facts, such as 'Myths and facts on immigration'[8]. Anti-sexist exercises may make use of employment statistics, media images or extracts from *The Naked Ape in The Guardian*.

In integrated humanities, however, far more is required than using varying types of awareness programmes. A general resource review is essential, and two important checklists, particularly concentrating on racism are *Ten Quick Ways Ways to Analyze Children's Books for Racism and Sexism* (Council on Inter-Racial Books for Children, New York) and the *World Council of Churches Criteria* described in the Children's Book Bulletin of June 1979. Teacher unions such as the NUT have also published guidelines, and the spring 1985 copy of *Issues in Race and Education* has an excellent series of suggestions and reviewing techniques. With regard to literature a very useful source of reviews is the 'Letterbox Library', a club specializing in non-sexist, multicultural books (First floor, 5 Bradby Street, London, N16 8JN). Apart from obvious reviewing for bias, jargon and stereotyping, resource checklists include questions such as:

  (i) does the resource endorse European value, developments, concepts, lifestyles . . . exclusively?
 (ii) do these lifestyles appear as the norm and model for all peoples?
(iii) do other continents and peoples only come into the picture when they are 'discovered' by Europeans?

In terms of racism it is important to look at how minorities are seen — from an ethocentric majority viewpoint or from the minority standpoint. How many histories of North America use North American Indian history accounts written by white men rather than perhaps D. Brown's *Bury my Heart at Wounded Knee, An Indian History of the American West?*[9] How many books on surviving peoples such as the Inuit ('eskimos') or Australian aborigines concentrate on traditional and somewhat 'exotic' elements of their life-styles, whilst ignoring more recent conflict with western values? H. Brody's *The People's Land, Eskimos and Whites in the Eastern Arctic,*[10] is a rare exception to the seal-hunting, igloo-building eskimo 'glossies' used in schools.

A brief selection of resources on racism includes:

Auschwitz: Yesterday's Racism, London Auschwitz Education Committee, 1983;

Racism in the Workplace and Community, Unit P590, Open University Press, 1983;

Roots of Racism and *Patterns of Racism*, Insitute of Race Relations, 1982;

All Faiths for One Race, a race relations teaching pack edited by D. Ruddell and M. Phillips-Bell, 1982;

Resources for Multi-Cultural Education: An Introudction, edited by G. Klein, Longman for the Schools Council, 1982 — a resources guide.

But the resources, curriculum, awareness programmes and methods within integrated humanities present only a small part of the necessary change in schooling required by anit-racism and anti-sexism. Integrated humanities may simply be a good starting-off point for general staff awareness and changing social relations in the classroom. What is really needed in education is a total reappraisal of assumptions, goals and processes that are part of educational planning, and the acceptance that patriarchy and ethnocentrism are societal problems needing challenge rather than a conspiracy of silence. However the root issues derive from our own assumptions about the importance of racism and sexism in our society, and our own varying assumptions about the role and meaning of education programmes in changing social conditions. Teachers are faced with endless contradictions — working in an institutional system that in many ways perpetuates dominance and oppression, whilst themselves often sympathizing with the resentments of the oppressed.

There is little point, however, in being totally pessimistic about the power of schools to change society, for to be pessimistic is to be complacent. Schools *do* have a chance to issue challenges to the *status quo* and a chance to develop critical thinking in their students. Nobody will challenge society unless we can develop a degree of optimistic hope for changing it, be it by a gradual 'chipping away' or by a social revolution. The important factor is collective awareness of, and opposition to, the injustices of society.

Returning to the school curriculum, it is worth repeating that combating racism and sexism requires more than separate timetable slots in 'moral education', 'guidance' or 'pastoral/tutorial' sessions — or even in integrated humanities. It needs to become an accepted school policy to combat racism and sexism not just in words but through action. Thus cross-faculty teams and wide-reaching working parties are necessary, including representatives of all school members — caretaking, ancillary teaching staff and *students*. These bodies can seriously review the ethos, aims and hidden curriculum of the school rather than merely the academic management of a subject-bound curriculum. My recent research in Leicestershire schools undertaken as part of a Masters course at the University of Leicester School of Education found that these working parties are rarely as effective as intended by their initiators for various reasons, including conflicting political viewpoints, the complexity of terminology involved, apathy by the rest of the staff and power structures within schools, compounded by physical lack of time in already over-crowded teacher days.

For evidence of racism and sexism in society one could do worse than consider school staffing hierarchies. For example in the mid-1970s there were only 0.15 per cent teachers compared to 1.5 per cent pupils in England and Wales of West Indian origin.[11] Or, for example, there are many inner city schools with high proportions of black students, but few if any black staff, and considerable hierarchical disparity. Heads of faculty, principals and vice principals tend to be white and generally male, whether in inner city schools or elsewhere. Patriarchy and ethnocentrism is only too apparent in the status and number of teachers in the school management hierarchy. The 'mothering role' is continued to be taken by 'dinner ladies', school nurses and pastoral staff but there are comparatively few female caretakers — or women in the upper eschelons of school management.

Patriarchy and ethnocentrism require a great deal of thought, a great deal of time, a complete change of attitudes, considerable resource review, a radical change in staffing and promotion policy and a direct political challenge. Integrated humanities should certainly be playing an essential key role in this challenge, but it cannot move forward alone: it must take the rest of education along with it.

Notes

1 LONDON BOROUGH OF BRENT EDUCATION COMMITTEE (1983) *Education for a Multi-Cultural Democracy*, London, Brent Education Committee
2 KIDRON, M and SEGAL, S (1981) *State of the World Atlas*, London, Pluto Press
3 WRIGHT, D (1983) in *Geography Education Journal*, V, May
4 SPENDER, D (1982) *Invisible Women: The Schooling Scandal*, London, Writers and Readers
5 BEDDIS, R (1982) *Sense of Place*, Oxford, Oxford University Press
6 TWITCHIN, J and DEMUTH, C (1981) *Multicultural Education*, London, BBC Publications
7 UNESCO (1979) *An Experience Centred Curriculum, Educational Studies and Documents, No 17*, London, HMSO
8 COMMISSION FOR RACIAL EQUALITY (1981) 'Myths and facts on immigration' in HICKS, D *Minorities: A Teaching Resource Book for the Multiethnic Curriculum*, London, Heinemann
9 Published in 1975 by Picador
10 Published in 1975 by Pelican
11 SELECT COMMITTEE ON RACE RELATIONS AND IMMIGRATION (1977).

Strategies for Curriculum Change: How to Implement an Integrated Humanities Course

Den Corrall

Many of the teachers now attempting to introduce integrated humanities courses went to university or college during the sixties or early seventies. They started teaching at a time of relative expansion and interest in new ideas in education. Amongst the more radical ideas was a belief in open and, as far as possible in a school, democratic decision-making. One of the ironies of the present situation is that the exercise of democracy in many staff rooms may now actually thwart rather than instigate innovations such as integrated humanities.

This chapter attempts to offer strategies and tactics for teachers keen to introduce integrated humanities while maintaining a commitment to open decision-making in schools where the majority of staff are generally hostile, or at best apathetic, towards such a course. It makes two assumptions in common with all other contributors to this symposium. The first is that integrated humanities, in some form or other, is a good thing, and all schools should have such a course. The second is that active participation in decision-making is a fundamental aim of all such courses and they would therefore fit uneasily into an authoritarian or autocratic school.

What follows is an expanded version of a brief talk given at the autumn 1984 DES East Midlands Regional Course 'Integrated humanities in the core curriculum' held in Leicestershire. In our original plan for this course we had not planned an item on how to implement integrated humanities courses. It was only included on the second day by popular demand. During the first day many of those attending said that they wanted a course like integrated humanities in their schools, but did not know how to overcome certain difficulties.

The main obstacles to implementation seemed to be one, or

combinations, of the following: reluctant or hostile heads, 'traditional' heads of department, or staff who were unwilling to change. In response to this request for help, the following was offered as a practical guide to implementing curriculum change. It represents no more than one person's experience during fifteen years of teaching in three secondary schools with different philosophies, age-ranges, and styles of decision-making ranging from autocratic to open.

It needs to be said at the outset that an individual's ability to implement change is, in most schools, related to that person's position in the hierarchy of scale points and posts of responsibility. It is, generally speaking, easier for a head to instigate innovation than for a scale 1 teacher, and the following strategies must be seen in that context.

Strategies

Three ways of innovating are:

(i) by dictat from a person or group in a senior position, for example a head, senior management team, governors, or the local education authority;

(ii) by bringing proposals to formally constituted faculty, department, or staff meetings;

(iii) by forming working groups of committed people who will eventually report, with proposals, to the head or formally constituted committee.

I would like to argue that the third of these is best, because it is both effective and open.

To most teachers, whose view of life was created by the radical sixties, the dictat method is an anathema. It is difficult to encourage young people to be active participants in a democratic society if neither they, nor their teachers, have an effective say in how school is run.

Also, experience shows that an innovation, such as the implementation of an integrated humanities course, will fail if it is imposed from above, because staff will be resentful, there will be a suspicion of manipulation, and, in the end, the idea is unlikely to work because the people whose idea it was will not be the ones who teach it. A course like this will only succeed if there are staff with sufficient enthusiasm and commitment to its aims and objectives. It is not good enough for a head nervously contemplating his falling rolls to instruct a long-serving head of department to develop an integrated course in return for a promotion.

It may seem like a blow against the ideal of open decision-making to reject the use of formally constituted committees or meetings as a strategy for innovation. However, in the three very different schools I have taught in, the staff meeting, and the department and faculty meetings have all, on various occasions, halted innovation and been a conservative force in the school. The two main reasons for this are: that proposals for innovation often come to such meetings in an ill-thought-out and half-baked form, and that such meetings act as a forum for those staff who are either not interested or opposed to change to influence the final decision. This is not an argument against democracy. Clearly in a situation of open decision-making one has to accept that not every decision will be the one you support, but it is unwise to have good ideas rejected at staff meetings because of poor tactics or bad presentation.

The best long-term strategy is to set up a working group of committed people. At Bosworth College, Leicestershire, numerous working parties were set up to examine problems or to develop new initiatives. Their brief was always to make recommendations to the general staff meeting. The most successful were those composed of staff with a commitment to the particular innovation. The least successful were those composed of representatives from different staff room factions, departments and differing points of view. Most of the latter type never produced proposals because they could not even agree on what they were supposed to be doing. Indeed on one of these unsuccessful working parties some senior staff admitted that their only reason for attending was to ensure that no recommendations to alter the *status quo* should be made — a position they could just as easily have argued for at the full staff meeting when the working party's recommendations were presented.

The working groups that did successfully initiate innovation were those composed solely of staff with a commitment to the development of a new idea. A good example was a small group who, in the mid-seventies, developed a course called human ecology which aimed to encourage fourth and fifth year students to actively study environmental issues under the themes of population, food, shelter, pollution and resources on local, national and global levels, taught by teams of teachers drawn from science, design and humanities faculties.

This group arose from casual staff room conversation. Some of us began to realize that certain issues such as food production and distribution, or the exploitation of the world's resources could not properly be studied by consigning them to separate subject and department pigeon holes. From that starting point a group of individuals from the science, design and humanities faculties began to meet in pubs and in each other's houses. Despite opposition from some staff within those faculties, the group developed and resourced the course, got it accepted as an option subject and successfully negotiated with examination boards to get it accepted as a Mode 3 'O' level and CSE. Members of the group then went on to team-teach the course in what, at the time, was and probably still today is, a unique exercise in integrated learning.

Some of the lessons learned by this group proved useful when in the late seventies another equally committed group integrated core design with core humanities (which already included English) to form a more coherent and, we believed, more exciting core learning experience for fourth and fifth years.

The significant fact about both of these examples is that the working groups came into existence not at the behest of the head or senior management team, nor because formally constituted bodies like the staff or faculty meetings had decided more integration would be a good thing. They came into existence, and were ultimately successful, because a group of teachers, who really represented nobody but themselves, decided to develop an idea they believed in, then presented it to the rest of the staff and the important decision-making bodies, at the right time and in an acceptable form.

This final part of the process, presenting your idea so that significant numbers of the rest of the staff are convinced is clearly crucial. So we need now to move from *strategy* and consider *tactics*.

Tactics

This is offered as a practical guide to the tactics of curriculum change, based on experience rather than rigorous research. Clearly a teacher's position in the school hierarchy of scale points and posts of responsibility will often determine his or her ability to influence curriculum development, but there is a great deal that the ordinary classroom teacher can do if he or she is determined. David Hargreaves in *The Challenge for the Comprehensive School*[1], suggests that it is young, new teachers who are most likely to challenge the present curriculum orthodoxies and it is they who we should encourage and look to for new initiatives. He is right, but there are also a great many teachers at all levels in schools who see the need for change, but are daunted by the inertia, apathy and stick-in-the-mud attitudes of other colleagues, particularly senior staff.

The following is a series of tactics that might be appropriate:

1   Cultivate Useful People

The useful people for the cause of integrated humanities will vary from school to school, but I would suggest that in all schools no innovation such as this will get off the ground unless the timetabler and, to a lesser degree, the pastoral people have been won over, or, at least, neutralized.

The member of staff who writes the timetable is, in many ways, the most influential person in the school. The working life of all staff, students and ancilliaries is determined by this person's work. He or she has the power to influence what subjects are blocked together, which teams of teachers will be together at any given time, the use of rooms, and allocations of time. In many schools this power may be circumscribed by: discussion, the recommendations of various groups and committees or department heads. In the end, though, the final timetable is the work of one person who has to balance many conflicting demands of which curriculum innovation may be only one amongst a series of otherwise pragmatic decisions that have to be taken. If the timetabler is not interested in, or unsympathetic to integrated humanities, the following courses of action may be necessary:

(i)   Become familiar with the workings of the timetable. Your group should become experts on how the timetable is drawn up and operates.

(ii) In your plan for integrated humanities, you must demonstrate how it works on the timetable. It is no good coming up with a wonderful scheme that cannot be fitted into a timetable.

(iii) Be prepared for the obvious limitations that the timetabler will throw at you. These will probably include difficulties with rooms. Most schools were not built with suites of open-plan rooms tailor made for team taught integrated work with facilities for every activity from modelling to video recording. Also there is nowadays very little money available to schools to make costly building alterations. So you must have a clear idea about how the scheme will work within the existing buildings.

Another difficulty will be your proposed use of staff. You may have an idea about which teachers will make the best teams in each year, but the timetabler and their department head may have plans for them elsewhere. Also if you are introducing your scheme with an integrated team of teachers in one year, this may limit their availability to teach in other years. Integrated teams mean teachers giving more periods to a class in one year.

Department heads also need to be consulted about use of their department's staff. They, and the timetabler, should also be consulted if you are proposing altering the time allocation for subjects. Unless you have got backing from the rest of the staff for a major timetable change it is probably tactful and sensible to propose timetabling the new integrated humanities course in the time available on the timetable for the single subjects it will replace. For instance if an integrated humanities course is proposed to replace two forty-minute history lessons, two forty-minute geography lessons and a forty-minute religious education lesson it would cause the timetabler fewer problems if you propose an integrated humanities course that takes up the equivalent of five forty-minute lessons.

In schools with a highly developed pastoral system the pastoral heads are often influential members of staff. It is therefore a good idea to get them on your side. One of the strong arguments for integrated courses, not just humanities, is that they increase the amount of time that a teacher can spend with a particular group. This means the teacher will know a particular set of individual students much better. This will increase the likelihood of good relationships developing and lead to more effective pastoral work. Two examples will illustrate the point.

At Bosworth we very quickly realized that in the fourth and fifth year a student's humanities teacher probably knew him or her better than their pastoral tutor, quite simply because the humanities teacher worked with the student for six forty-five minute lessons in the week, often doing English and drama work that revealed much about the student's ideas, personality and background, whereas the pastoral tutor only saw the student for five twenty-minute sessions when registers had to be marked, notices given out and many other administrative tasks performed.

At Hamilton, my present school, the staff developed a humanities course in the first year that got over this problem. The course integrates social studies, English and religious education, takes up thirteen forty-five minute periods and is taught by a team of teachers who are also first year tutors. This has the added advantage of making a good bridge between the primary school experience, where pupils have one teacher for pretty well all of their lessons in the week and the secondary experience with its emphasis on specialist teaching which involves pupils being taught by many different teachers in the week.

Pastoral heads are always looking for ways of improving relationships and effective pastoral work. An integrated humanities course offers this possibility, especially if the teachers can also be the pastoral tutors. This is clearly easier to argue for in an horizontal than in a vertical pastoral system.

2   Gather Evidence of Good Practice from Other Schools

Selective use of examples of successful humanities teaching from other schools can often be useful when presenting the case. In particular it is important to gather evidence of good examination results where students are following humanities courses. Although integrated humanities teachers would argue that their courses are intended to give students much more than an examination certificate at the end, they are sufficiently realistic to realize that in the upper school no new course really has much chance of being introduced or surviving for the whole range of ability of students if it cannot produce as good, if not better, examination results than those produced by the courses it replaced. Fortunately, over the past fifteen years humanities teachers have been in the forefront of developing Mode 3 syllabuses at CSE, 'O' level and now 16+, that encourage desirable educational goals that are broader than many traditional examination syllabuses.

It is very important for the continued development of integrated humanities that such courses are offered to the whole ability range. Too often in the past they have been seen as courses for the less able while the more able get on with their history and geography.

3   Anticipate Problems with Parents, Governors and Other Departments in the School

The possibility of problems arising from these quarters will vary tremendously from one school to another. The important thing is to anticipate them.

As a general rule it is better to be entirely open and to keep all parties well informed of plans for change once the ideas have been well formulated. It is better to deal with objections before the new courses starts than to have to face major criticisms, particularly from people who feel they were not properly consulted in the first place, when the course is in operation.

At Bosworth we faced a fair amount of criticism from some parents in the early stages of the humanities course because English was integrated in the course and therefore did not appear on their sons' and daughters' timetable. We could have avoided this if the course had been better explained to parents and if it could have been demonstrated that the quality, breadth and depth of English work — reading, writing and oral work — encouraged by the course was at worst comparable and at best better than they would have found on non-integrated English courses.

Governor's reactions to such a course will vary greatly and it is important to come up with appropriate responses to criticisms and queries. The most common problem that governors will identify is that of political bias. 'If you are teaching pupils about political and social issues how will you avoid bias?'

This is the worst question to answer, because although we would like to reply that most teaching contains bias and that it is really impossible to teach most subjects in school in a value-free way, that response is not really understood by governors and other outsiders who still believe that there is 'balance' and that teaching can be unbiased. The only reply to this question that seems to placate most critics is that teachers will make it clear when 'a point of view is being expressed'.

Some governors, especially those appointed by political parties, actively welcome such courses because they believe that the school should be encouraging political education and social awareness. Such governors obviously need to be cultivated.

Other departments, and their heads, may raise objections if they feel threatened by the new course. Particular objections may be: to 'poaching' of time for integrated humanities from their subjects, questions of overlap in content of courses, and in some cases it may be that they will blame integrated humanities for student liveliness more usually referred to as 'lack of discipline'. In some schools members of other departments complain that because students are encouraged to question, discuss and generally be an active participant in humanities lessons, they are more difficult to teach in lessons where passive, uncritical learning is required.

Patient staff room discussion, and occasional compromise on questions of time allocation and content overlap, can usually overcome the first two objections. There is, however, no easy answer to the charge of 'lively students' — except to offer the platitude that good schools encourage a variety of teaching styles and learning experiences.

4   Don't Propose Anything Until it is Thoroughly Worked Out and Explained in Detail

The art is to find a middle line between, on the one extreme a half-baked, ill-thought-out proposal, and on the other a complicated package worked out to the finest detail. You will probably have only one chance to propose your new course to the staff, relevant committee or head. It is therefore crucial to get it right. An ill-thought-out scheme, with many timetable and staffing problems will probably be rejected with at best the request to go away, think about it and come back another year when it has been better thought out. At worst it may put back the cause of integrated humanities for many years.

The other extreme — a finely detailed blue print — may not allow for the rest of the staff to make modifications and to feel part of the development. Other staff will feel committed to a new idea if it looks well thought out, if it doesn't threaten them too much, if they feel they have had some say in the final stages of its development and, most important of all, if they understand it and its relevance.

5   Start With One Year — Preferably a Year Where Staff Generally Agree There Are Problems

An example from Hamilton will illustrate this tactic.

It was generally agreed at a staff conference that there were 'problems with our second year'. A great deal of effort and imagination had gone into radically altering the first, fourth and fifth year curriculum, but the second and third years had been neglected. In the second year the curriculum was divided into traditional subjects. In the humanities faculty this meant a separation into history and geography courses plus a single religious education period.

Taking advantage of this general staff dissatisfaction a small group of staff, committed to the principle of greater integration and cohesion, set to work to revamp the second year so that there was greater integration between all subjects, not just within the humanities faculty. At the time of writing the working group is still deliberating.

Although it is probably practical to work on a year at a time, it is important to bear in mind two important considerations. The first is that there should be an overall idea of the skills, concepts and content taught in humanities courses, or any other integrated course, in all the years of the school. One year's course cannot be planned in isolation from the courses that operate, or might at some future date operate, in other years of the school. The second is that it can sometimes happen that a group of committed teachers exhaust themselves planning, arguing for, resourcing, then teaching a new course in one year to such an extent that they find it difficult to sustain the momentum into other years where, perhaps less committed staff have to be recruited to teach and develop the new course.

6   *Use New Appointments to Get in Teachers Committed to the*
     Principle of Integrated Humanities

There are, unfortunately, severe limitations on the possibility of implementing this one. The first is that you have to be in a position to be
able to have some say in staff appointments. If you are not part of the
decision-making, you can at least take every opportunity to point out to
the head and other decision-makers that falling rolls mean that schools
will increasingly have to employ staff who can teach a range of subjects
rather than narrow specialisms. The second is the rather comic situation
that falling rolls mean schools will be able to make fewer appointments,
just at the time contraction of the curriculum is forcing some heads
to look more favourably at integration for purely pragmatic
reasons.

7   *Encourage Staff who Might be Receptive to Integrated*
     Humanities to Go Out on Courses and to Visit Other Schools

Most staff come back from courses and visits to other schools with their
horizons broadened. Even those who are unreceptive at least come back
with some knowledge of what integration is all about and staff room
discussions should be livelier as a result.

8   *Be Prepared for Apparent Muddle for a Time*

The first year of a new course or innovation will inevitably throw up
endless problems. By November of the first term it may very well seem
like utter chaos, and, to make matters worse, 'I told you so' will be
echoing round the staff room from the armchair critics. There is no easy
remedy for this, except thick skin and gritted teeth. Two essentials are:
to keep clearly in mind the principles and aims you believed to be right
when you started planning the course, and for those involved to
give each other personal support. It is essential to keep working as a
team.

What appears as 'muddle' may not be such a bad thing anyway. It is
more exciting and lively for students and staff to be in a situation where
there are no immediate answers to problems and where new situations
are regularly thrown up. This is, in some ways, a healthier atmosphere
to be in, than one where the work of the school goes on unchanged from
one year to the next.

9 *Try to Get Financial or Staffing Help from Outside the School*

This is really a long shot, but if the opportunity arises it is worth a try. There are outside agencies prepared to finance curriculum innovation and heads will not usually turn their nose up at money coming into the school. A good example is Groby Community College in Leicestershire which received a large amount of money from UNESCO to finance its world studies course — an integrated humanities course with a heavy emphasis on teaching about development. There are also many outside commercial institutions and educational trusts who regularly give prizes for curriculum innovation and school-based projects. Winning a prize and the attendant publicity gives immediate respectability and acceptance to a new course. The turning point for the integrated humanities and design core course at Bosworth came when it won first prize in a national competition organized by 'Education for Capability'. It is a good idea to enter your course, or individual projects undertaken by students, for every relevant competition you come across.

10 *Demonstrate that the New Course Might Fit Well With Other Innovations such as TVEI, Profiling and HMI's 'Curriculum 11–16' booklet. Mention David Hargreaves Somewhere in your plans!*

Many bandwagons are rolling in education at the moment. Some of them like TVEI have not found favour with many humanities teachers, but they cannot be ignored. Integrated humanities has much to offer schools wishing to develop profiling schemes, because it emphasizes skills and encourages students to appraise their own work.

Other contributors to this symposium will show how integrated humanities courses can very successfully cover many of the eight areas of experience that HMI argue in the booklet *Curriculum 11–18* should be essential ingredients of the core curriculum. Hargreaves in *The Challenge for the Comprehensive School*[2] argues that community studies should also be an essential element of the core in the secondary school. Community studies is a major part of most integrated humanities courses. Both the HMI booklet and the Hargreaves book have been extremely widely read by heads and other teachers, and have received a generally favourable response. Indeed they are arguably the two most important statements on comprehensive education to have emerged in the past few years. Therefore any proposal for an integrated humanities course ought to quote from them and draw heavily on their suggestions.

Finally a brief word on TVEI — really to make a point about bandwagon jumping. Don't jump on *any* one that happens to come along. Humanities teachers will not easily give up certain principles. One of them is that vocational training has little place in the secondary school. They believe instead, that encouraging students to think for themselves, to take a critical look at the world around them, and to recognize when they are being 'conned' by the media, employers, politicians and, for that matter teachers, is a more useful preparation for life after school than being instructed in a vocational skill that will be no use to them, or could just as easily have been taught after they have left school.

Having said all that — it is the case that one large upper school in Leicestershire did use the extra resources and challenge to the existing curriculum which TVEI brought to introduce an integrated humanities course in the core in their fourth and fifth year.

Common Sense and Living Dangerously

It is important to make two final points that really go beyond tactics and strategy.

The first is that you must convince staff that the new course will be better than what has gone on before. Within a couple of years of its implementation it is important to demonstrate clearly observable ways in which the student's education is better with the new course. Examination results in the upper school are clearly important here — but other things should be emphasized such as an improvement in students' social awareness, in their ability to research and interpret information, in their motivation and enjoyment of that particular section of the school curriculum, and in their willingness to discuss and participate in school life and the community.

Exhibitions of work can help convince staff. At Bosworth we always used to display students' projects so that staff from other departments could see the work that had been done.

The second point brings us back to where we started. In the end, no new scheme will survive unless the majority of staff are with you. It is better to make compromises than to insist on an all-or-nothing scheme that is resented by substantial sections of the staff. Getting a limited scheme accepted is better than no scheme at all; at least the beginnings of integrated humanities will be there on the timetable and can be built on in future years.

Den Corrall

Those were the common sense points. I would like to end though with an encouragement to live dangerously. Take a few risks. Schools can easily become too cosy and comfortable, reflecting a society that is becoming more conservative and interested in tradition. Schools should challenge this mood. Integrated humanities *does* threaten 'traditional subjects' where this really means long-established teaching methods, and this is no bad thing.

Notes

1 HARGREAVES, D (1982) *The Challenge for the Comprehensive School*, London, Routledge and Kegan Paul.
2 *Ibid*

Geography and Integration

Vivien Keller

Over the last ten to fifteen years interdisciplinary and multidisciplinary humanities courses have begun to establish themselves on the secondary school timetable. Integration is at the heart of contemporary progressive education. However, there are many history, geography, economics and social studies teachers who feel professionally disturbed by the move and, more importantly, believe that integration offers at best a second rate course that lacks the academic rigour of traditional single subjects. History and geography have well-established places in the school curriculum that date back to at least the end of the last century. Both subjects have developed and undergone many changes in philosophy and pedagogy. Today the most progressive courses have responded to a need for a stimulating, relevant, questioning and problem-solving approach that will enable students to understand and make rational decisions about the very complex adult world they will find themselves in. Teachers of such courses aim to provide students with transferable skills. However, this is not necessarily apparent to the student. An integrated approach can demonstrate and encourage skill transferability and provide students with an holistic approach that is essential for a full understanding of contemporary issues.

Many contemporary issues facing society like nuclear war, world inequality, environmental destruction, unemployment and rapid urbanization cannot be fully understood when studied through the models and theories of a single discipline. Geography teachers are beginning to find that 'an honest explanation of patterns and processes often demand economic and social or political understanding!'.[1] Single subject specialists are often restricted by their own academic background. Some geographers have only limited social, economic and political awareness. Equally some sociologists' perception of the interaction of the human/ physical environment will be superficial. An integrated approach which draws upon the expertise and skills of single subjects is essential in a curriculum which aims to provide students with an understanding of the human condition. When integrated courses are developed with teams of teachers from various disciplines who have similar progressive educational philosophies, the course can be rich and vibrant with cross-fertilization of skills, methodologies and information. Collaborative and enquiry-based methods inevitably cross single subject boundaries. Geography teachers who believe in developing a questioning approach to the spatial patterns, processes and models they deal with have an important part to play in this development.

This chapter is primarily concerned with the relationship of geography as an option subject and core integrated humanities during the examination years in a secondary school. Progressive geography teaching and integrated humanities can be mutually supportive. The MEG integrated humanities syllabus is free of specified factual content and places much emphasis upon the acquisition of skills. These skills can be used to enhance a geography student's awareness and understanding of human response to the physical environment.

Geography in the Secondary Curriculum

Geography appears on the timetable of most secondary schools. Prior to the 1960s it often existed as an easily identifiable subject throughout most of the school years. It emerged as a school subject at the end of the nineteenth century to teach pupils about the Empire.

> The colonies of England, her commerce, her emigrations, her wars, her missionaries and her scientific explorers bring her into contact with all parts of the globe, and it is therefore a matter of imperial importance that no reasonable means should be neglected of training her youth in sound geographical knowledge.[2]

Geography today, however, is no longer the 'capes and bays' knowledge of the last century. In many schools the learner is not expected to accumulate teacher-directed facts and descriptions. In its place a student-centred, interactive approach has been developed. This stresses the use of problem-solving techniques which provide students with the skills that will enable them to make sense of human response to the physical environment. It was during the 1960s and 1970s that the 'new' geography was established and during the 1980s a more humanistic approach is beginning to appear.

The 'new' geography was concerned with a search for theory. Thus statistics, models and systems-analysis were introduced. The approach placed great emphasis on the skills that would enable students to interpret and analyze processes, patterns and relationships. Less emphasis was placed on factual recall. Humanistic geography however involves a move away from the impersonal theory of the 1960s to a more personal view of the environment. Students are encouraged to think about their mental images of the world and their own attitudes and behaviour in it. This approach places equal emphasis on knowledge and skills acquisition and on values.

Although there have been many changes in geography teaching since the 1960s, these changes have been more fundamental in some junior and lower secondary school years. Here geography is disappearing as a separate subject on the school timetable. Multidisciplinary and interdisciplinary approaches to humanities have been introduced. The *multidisciplinary* approach draws upon the content of history, geography, social studies and religious studies to develop courses. Such courses are often chronological and distinct subject areas can be identified in the curricular design. Those schools which have developed an *interdisciplinary* course draw upon the *skills* of the traditional humanities subjects in order for students to gain an understanding of a particular theme, problem or area of study. The separate disciplines cannot be identified.

Many Leicestershire high schools (10–14) have been particularly influenced by the work of Jerome Bruner. His curriculum philosophy is based upon the idea of a 'spiral curriculum'. His social science approach had the effect of excluding much traditional high school humanities subject matter and concentrated upon developing materials which have helped students understand the 'human condition' The Bruner package called 'Man: A Course of Study' (MACOS) was introduced into several Leicestershire high schools and has had a considerable influence on teaching techniques, approaches and content matter. Although many schools have begun to move on in curriculum terms, the philosophy and approach of MACOS still has some influence. The schools that have used, or are currently using, MACOS have generally developed a child-centred approach in which mixed ability teaching is commonplace.

Teachers are relatively free from examination constraints with lower secondary school students. Thus the progressive move away from traditional discipline studies is made easier. Unfortunately the final years of secondary humanities education are locked into an examination system that is based upon traditional disciplines and is very slow to change. Examinations have exerted a crucial influence on the secondary school curriculum. They affect timetabling, pupil motivation and teaching techniques. Both students and teachers can become trapped in a 'vicious circle' of examination monotony. Figure 1, illustrating this 'vicious circle', is based on the Schools Council publication *Geography 14–18: A Handbook For Curriculum Development*.

Figure 1

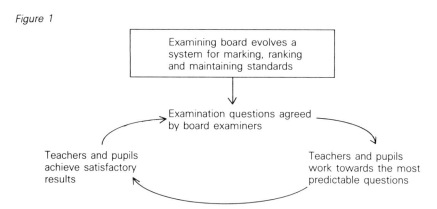

Schools are very aware of students' and parents' need for public examination 'satisfaction'. Whether the schools teach single subject humanities courses or an integrated approach one of their aims will be to prepare students for public examinations and further academic study. The body of knowledge established by the examination board can become of paramount importance in the schools' teaching. The examination curriculum has been involved in the establishment of *factual content*. The teaching of skills, processes and patterns have been incidental to the main task. Such examination 'straight-jackets' exist in all the humanities subjects.

In a traditional geography examination syllabus, classroom teaching would be dictated by a broad (and sometimes not so broad!) indication of the content to be imparted and past examination questions would guide decisions about the range of examples, depth of treatment and style of questions to be covered. In turn, these would influence students' perception of what was expected of them. In short, the form of the examination and the examination questions became the curriculum. Thus geography suffered from teacher-dominated, fact-imparting courses which were aimed at student success in the public examinations. Such courses usually involved regional studies, OS mapwork, geomorphology and meteorology/climatology. The processes, patterns, interrelationships and underlying concepts were rarely stressed.

When the school leaving age was raised to 16, the Schools Council was instrumental in introducing new curriculum ideas for those students in their final years in compulsory education who would normally have left without taking a public examination. The *Geography for the Young School Leaver Project* (GYSL) was introduced for these less able students and at the same time the *Geography 14–19 (Bristol) Project* was funded for the more able. GYSL was concerned with developing a package that would be relevant and stimulating for the young school leaver, whilst the *Geography 14–19 (Bristol) Project* aimed to introduce in schools the theory of the 'new' geography that was being developed in the universities. Since their introduction the two projects have come closer together. The more recent joint certification syllabuses associated with these developments are beginning to have an increasing effect upon geography examination teaching. However, reorganization of examination boards and the introduction of the common system of examining at 16+ and its related 'national criteria' could influence such developments.

Schools still using fact-laden syllabuses view geography as a range of factual content that needs to be acquired by the student. The MEG (Midlands Examining Group) integrated humanities syllabus on the other hand is not concerned with factual content but with underlying *skills*. Thus teachers who could not see beyond 'content' and who, like certain examination boards, believe there is something sacrosanct about such 'content', would have little to contribute to a skills-based integrated humanities course. However, geography teachers, like those in other disciplines, have begun to think more deeply about the way in which effective learning takes place and, equally important, the relevance of their teaching. The most recent moves in geography have been away from the theorizing introduced in the 1960s and 1970s to a more radical and humanistic approach. 'People-oriented' courses are being encouraged by the Schools Council *16–19 Geography Project* and it is to be hoped that this Project's approach will have some influence on the common system of examination at 16+ in geography.

This combination of skills-learning and a humanistic approach is very much in keeping with the philosophy and aims of the MEG integrated humanities syllabus. Such developments enable geography to coexist as well as become an integral part of a 'core' humanities course. The skills acquired can be shown to be transferable. One area of study is concerned with human response to the natural environment and the other with the total concept of 'humanity'. The desire for relevance and an increased awareness of the need for an understanding of the human situation or condition has encouraged changes in many areas of the humanities curriculum. Teachers involved in these developments are beginning to see the logic of integration.

The Role of Geography as an Option Subject and Part of a 'Core' Humanities Course at Hind Leys Community College, Leicestershire

In many secondary schools geography is administered through a separate department that either works in isolation or within a faculty structure. Although integration may occur in the lower years the examination constraints already outlined and the tradition of geography teaching has meant the continuation of separate departments and the use, wherever possible, of specialist staff during the public examination years.

Most upper schools in Leicestershire organize their curriculum and timetables around 'faculties'. At Hind Leys Community College geography is a department within the humanities faculty. Other departments within the faculty include history, sociology, business studies, economics and typing. Each department has a teacher responsible for its organization and each of these subjects is optional. At the centre of the faculty is a 'core' integrated humanities course based on the MEG integrated humanities syllabus. The head of faculty is responsible for the organization and development of this, along with contributions from single subject specailists. Geography and history are popular examination options.

Case 1 — Geography as an Option

Since 1983 the geography department has used the Schools Council *14–18 Geography Project* joint certification syllabus (EMREB/ Cambridge Examination Boards). Although the syllabus is fairly recent as a 'joint certification' course it is based on the original Schools Council 'O' level examination. The fundamental aim of the joint certification syllabus is 'to enable pupils to use important skills, ideas and models drawn on in geography to classify and interpret such everyday experiences as discerning order in a landscape and bring regional and world problems into appropriate frames of reference'.[3]

The geographical skills and ideas advocated in this syllabus include: the use of maps, including ordnance survey maps, systems analysis, models, decision-making exercises and an understanding of the underlying processes that could result in or bring about change in the landscape and spatial patterns. Individual schools or groups of schools working as consortia are expected to plan their own curricula based on the following table:

TABLE 1:   *The Structure of the Core Syllabus (taken from the Cambridge/EMREB examination regulations for joint certification in geography)*

A *Illustrative examples to be chosen from*	B *Wider systems or contexts to be considered*	C *Appropriate distribution of examples chosen*
(i) Weather and climate	Atmospheric and oceanic circulation	Local and British Isles 40–50 per cent approx
(ii) Contrasting landforms	Longer-term geologic and shorter-term geomorphic processes	
(iii) Conservation of natural resources	Hydrologic cycle	Other developed regions of the world 15–30 per cent approximately
(iv) Agricultural land-use		
(v) Location, growth and decline of industries	Physical ⎤ processes influen-	
(vi) Transport networks	Techno- cing	Less developed regions of the world 15–30 per cent approximately
(vii) Economic growth and trade	logical spatial patterns	
(viii) Settlement patterns between and within towns	Economic ⎰ and land-	Wider physical and economic systems at a world scale 10–15 per cent approximately
(ix) Population growth and distribution	Social scapes Political	

A rather hefty 60 per cent of the final examination mark consists of a terminal, differentiated examination paper. Students can be entered for one of two available papers: one is aimed at the able student who is capable of achieving 'O' level standard and the other at those who are expected to gain CSE grades. The examination content is based upon the illustrative examples outlined in the core syllabus. However the examination is primarily skills-based and students can draw on a range of illustrative examples. The rest of the examination is assessed on performance in school-based assessment units. SBAs are designed by schools and used to assess work which cannot be undertaken in time-limited conditions. The work could be about a topic of particular interest to a teacher or student or is specifically related to the school's local area. Each student needs to complete one unit of work of each of the following areas of study: a regional or synoptic study, a study of the physical environment, a planning problem and an individual study. Each of the units are designed to encourage the use of geographical skills and theories as well as stressing the interrelationship of humans and the physical environment.

Ideally a student-centred, enquiry approach should not place such emphasis on a time-limited terminal examination. However, the course is relatively factual-content free and is concerned with the development of skills and enquiry methods. There is freedom for a wide range of classroom and field study experience and an opportunity to stress the underlying processes. Illustrative examples can be drawn for topical and 'teenage'-relevant issues and events. The course can be as relevant and stimulating as the teacher wishes, or is able, to make it.

Case 2 — Geography-Related Work in the Integrated Course

The course described above coexists well with the 'core' integrated humanities. Both courses intend to encourage learner autonomy and both stress the role of independent enquiry and research. They have similar philosophies and pedagogic styles. All teaching groups are mixed ability and all geography specialist teachers teach and take part in planning the integrated humanities curriculum. The geographical skills and knowledge acquired during geography lessons can be used to enhance students' understanding of issues and themes being tackled in integrated humanities. The reverse also occurs, skills are demonstrated to be mutually supportive and transferable.

Hind Leys College has had a core integrated humanities course since the College opened in 1977. The present course concerns itself with important contemporary issues and draws upon several methodologies and perspectives in order for a full appraisal of a particular issue to be achieved. The areas of study are meant to involve students using research techniques that will require locating and selecting information from a variety of sources. The skills and methodologies used during this research can be drawn from any of the traditional humanities subject areas. In order to facilitate this, core humanities teachers work, wherever possible, in teams of four or five with mixed subject specialisms. Each member of staff contributes his/her particular expertise and knowledge to an area of study. The teams are primarily concerned with the organization and development of a curriculum for their group of students. The content or area of study may vary from team to team and reflects the interests of the teachers and the students they work with. The teams draw up a broad outline of the two-year course in which skills development and content (organizing ideas) are identified. However, because the course responds to the needs of the students, the content and order of skills teaching may change.

The school, as required by the MEG regulations for this syllabus, has written very broad integrated humanities 'exemplars' which allow flexibility and freedom, and while the syllabus lays down pairs of 'organizing ideas', the course does not require that each term we tackle a particular 'organizing idea'. Many contemporary issues that are being dealt with will draw upon several different 'organizing ideas'. A student investigating the public's response to famine relief in Ethiopia will concern herself with issues associated with *conflict and cooperation*, *prejudice and empathy* as well as *equality and inequality* (three of the MEG pairs of organizing ideas). Such a student may wish also to find out about *why* famine has occurred in East Africa or why there are food shortages in some parts of the world and surpluses in others. A student-centred course in which the teacher is the mediator and interpreter opens up many learning possibilities. The use of different subject-specialists within a team provides a wide range of personal experiences, knowledge and skills that can be tapped by the student.

Many of the same research skills are used in history, geography and integrated humanities. However a student is not permitted to submit the same unit of work for two different courses. During geography lessons a student may investigate, say, the effects of increased road traffic on the residents of Castle Donington after the expansion of the East Midlands airport. This unit of work could not be submitted for both geography and integrated humanities. Such a study may lead on to an investigation into changes in local employment structures since the expansion of the East Midlands airport or into the proposed development of a third London airport or something more topical like terrorist attacks on airports. Any of these would be included in the students' integrated humanities portfolio.

Following are two examples of units of study planned by a team of four teachers at Hind Leys College. The first example was taught during the first year of the examination course and the second was taught towards the end of the second year. Before each unit of work began the themes were discussed amongst the team and a general outline of possibilities developed, along with the skills that they expected the students to use or acquire. Note was also made of relevant 'organizing ideas' and possible range of study. Once an approach was decided upon the team pooled any resources they had available and where necessary wrote and acquired other relevant material. Many useful resources have been acquired and developed for 'core' humanities since 1977. (The original course was based upon Mode 3 CSE and 'O' level social studies examination syllabuses.) The resources of the core course as well as other departments in humanities were made available.

The themes and possible methodologies are always established during the introductory sessions. Introductory sessions can last from either one one-and-a-quarter hour lesson to a couple of weeks.

Vivien Keller

Example One

World of work   *Time: approx 8 weeks*

Identification of skills   This unit was taught fairly early in the first year of the examination course. Students had already been introduced and had practiced several research techniques. These included: social surveys, interviews (structured and unstructured), observation techniques, and some use of secondary resources like the booklets available in the faculty and videos and books in the school's resources centre. The team identified that the students had not had much experience of gaining information from the media, government statistics and developments, local community and, in particular, leading figures within that community. Although these areas where identified, the team did not expect all students to use all areas but wanted them to become aware of their possibilities. The team felt that a broad topic like 'work' would provide students with the possibilities for such skill development. Equally important it is a topic many student of this age come to feel concerned about and some students had begun taking part in work experience and community placement schemes and were beginning to gain some first-hand experience of employment.

Content Possibilities   The team decided to organize the 'content' under four headings and each member of staff was to take on responsibility for organizing and preparing resources associated with one heading. The areas of study were: (i) work in the community; (ii) the technological revolution in the workplace; (iii) trade unions; and (iv) work in the past.

When these headings were decided (they, to some extent, reflect the interests of the team members) the team was aware that one of the most important issues facing society today and of particular concern to young people was 'unemployment' and this had not been provided for in any obvious way under any of our four headings. The team had planned also a unit of work about 'poverty' and issues like unemployment, underemployment and low pay could be dealt with in that context. However, if a student wished to look more closely at local or regional unemployment within the topic of 'world of work' then he or she would be permitted to do so, we decided.

The team sub-divided the four areas of study in order to identify possible areas of research.

(i) Work in the community:

    (a) local employment structure and patterns;
    (b) local changes in industrial location;
    (c) work in a local knitwear factory;
    (d) government regional incentives for the Charnwood area;
    (e) the new industrial estate;
    (f) local opportunities for school leavers;
    (g) employment for women.

(ii) The technological revolution in the work place:

    (a) location of the electronics industry;
    (b) microtechnology and employment in the UK;
    (c) microtechnology in local industry;
    (d) education for new employment in the new industries;
    (e) the future?

(iii) Trade unions:

    (a) development of the trade union movement;
    (b) a study of the work of one local union branch;
    (c) study of a national union;
    (d) an industrial dispute, for example, the miners' strike or the teachers' pay claim;
    (e) government policy and attitude towards trade unions and trade union legislation.

(iv) Work in the past:

    (a) work in the local community fifty years ago;
    (b) origins and development of the local knitwear factories;
    (c) industrial revolution in the Midlands;
    (d) origins of trade unions;
    (e) child labour.

The above lists are not exhaustive, of course, and a different team of teachers would have arrived at different lists. Indeed the students themselves eventually offered other suggestions.

Once the team had established in their own minds possible areas of study and had gathered together enough resources to use during the introductory sessions and to provide at least a start for students' individual areas of research, they then had to decide upon classroom strategies.

Teaching strategy   The team thought it was important to build upon ideas and thoughts that the students already had about the world of work. Thus the introductory sessions were concerned with swapping ideas. In a classroom discussion students were encouraged to talk about their own experiences of work and to begin to think about the kinds of things that are likely to influence the work and the workplace. Each class group and its teacher began to identify possible areas of investigation and a list was drawn up on a blackboard or overhead projector. Some ideas such as 'the industrial revolution', 'microtechnology' and 'industrial location' needed brief explanation. The students were then encouraged to identify their own area of research.

During the following lessons resources, which included books, booklets, newspapers, wallcharts and videos were grouped under the four headings originally decided upon by the team. Each teacher made available, in her or his teaching room, the resources he or she had gathered. The students were made aware of the location of these resources and were encouraged to work alongside the particular member of staff whose resources would provide the most appropriate start to their investigation. The students' next task was to draw up a plan of their work and indicate the methodologies and resources they intended to use. Over the next few weeks students were contacting local employers and arranging factory, office, shop and farm visits. Some contacted local union representatives whilst others searched through the media for information about industrial disputes. Still others used books and resources in both the college and town library, as well as oral history, to investigate work in the past and some were mapping and surveying industrial activity on a new industrial estate. The final work could be communicated in a number of ways. These included the construction of wall charts, a report document, an imaginary radio broadcast or a short project. Students were encouraged to communicate their findings in an appropriate and interesting way. The work was very much student-centred, the teacher being there to encourage, guide and interpret.

Example Two

World inequality   *Time: approx 10 weeks*

Identification of skills   This unit of work was taught towards the end of the second examination year. By now students had been introduced to a wide range of research, investigation and problem-solving techniques and had tackled many individual, local and national issues. Prior to commencing this unit they had been introduced to the idea of international interdependency whilst studying issues associated with conflict, aggression and war as well as the moral issues associated with the arms race and nuclear warfare.

The main aim now was to encourage students to use their skills of interpretation and analysis to achieve some order out of the very complex global issue of inequality. The team was particularly concerned that the students should have more practice at the use and interpretation of national statistics, maps that displayed economic data, models of economic development and, most importantly, a re-evaluation and interpretation of their initial perceptions.

Content possibilities Although content possibilities were very broad the course, to begin with, was more teacher-directed than the previous example. Again working as a team the teachers planned and resourced the content of the unit. Much material was already available in humanities resources. The team limited the introductory sessions to the use of atlases, tables of national economic data, a *Global Report* video and a role-play exercise. Other resources were made available for a student investigation that was to come towards the end of the course.

Teaching strategy The team began by evoking students' responses to current media issues like famine in Ethiopia and the chemical disaster in India. Students were then encouraged to discuss their perceptions of life and living conditions in such countries. The following headings were provided in order to guide their discussions: (i) wealth; (ii) food; (iii) housing; (iv) education; (v) health; (vi) employment. Students were encouraged also to identify any interrelationships between these areas.

Once students had begun to realize the complexity of life in less-developed countries, they were introduced to world social and economic maps and national data of selected developed and less-developed countries. A series of structured questions were written in order to help students identify global, social and economic patterns and the inequalities that exist between nations. Next the *Global Report* video was shown and students discussed some of the problems and possible solutions that were outlined in the programme. The next stage was to encourage students to begin to view world inequality as a globally interrelated issue. This was achieved by the use of the role-play exercise *Star Power* which highlights the interplay of power between participants in solving the problem of the game.

When the initial problems and issues had been outlined, students had the opportunity to use any of the resources available within the faculty to undertake further study. The following areas were suggested:

(i) a regional study that investigated development strategies in Tanzania, India or Ghana;

(ii) an interdependence issue that could be associated with trade, multinational companies, aid or colonialism;

(iii) a thematic study about any of the following: less-developed world urbanization, the 'green revolution', exploitation of mineral resources, subsistence farming, plantations, landownership and reform, population pressures, industrialization and the role of women.

Available for the students was a list of books, booklets, videos and other resources they would find useful for their study. Most of the students communicated their ideas in a report.

These two examples are not offered as perfect practice but simply to illustrate the sort of 'geography-oriented' work that can be undertaken. Such work will vary from year to year responding to the needs of students and the teaching-teams. Some of it will be particularly interesting and stimulating and effective in encouraging appropriate skills and some less so. Work that may be successful with one group of teachers and students may not succeed in the same way with another. The MEG integrated humanities syllabus gives teachers freedom to reinterpret and generally rethink their approaches to issues and topics. The examination does not dictate the content or methods of skills teaching.

Research and investigation techniques and reappraisal and evaluation processes that are encouraged in core humanities can have far-reaching benefits for students, in both personal and academic terms, in many areas of the curriculum. At its very best it will equip students with a learning autonomy that enables them to make sense of a very complex world.

Problems and Successes of Geography and Integrated Humanities Coexistence

Hind Leys Community College opened with a 'core' humanities course and both feeder high schools (11–14) had established interdisciplinary approaches. Problems associated with establishing a 'core' using staff who were used to working in single subjects and parents and students used to a humanities timetable of separate history and geography did not exist. However problems have occurred. Although staff may be appointed to teach both integrated humanities and a single subject option, some have felt that their main responsibility should be towards the single subject and not the core because that is where their expertise is. Others have found the work-load associated with 'core' development excessive and believe that it is impossible to implement change in both the option course and the 'core' at the same time — and certainly resourcing and keeping up-to-date such resources for both the 'core' and an option subject can be very time-consuming. Some staff, again, have found it difficult to work in teams and have caused a limitation of the essential staff interaction.

Students and parents have generally responded well to the courses. They do not see any conflict between the core and single subject options. If a student takes courses in geography and integrated humanities she will very likely gain two worthwhile examination passes.

Also of some importance to the 'core' integrated humanities success is the purpose-built suite of rooms available to teach in. The classrooms are divided by moveable screens and there are offices and small classrooms off the main teaching area. Team-teaching and variation in group size are possible and easy to achieve. The humanities rooms are located also next to the College's resources centre. Thus student-centred, enquiry approaches are physically easy to arrange.

Coexistence of integrated humanities and geography can exist productively if supported by all concerned. More particularly they are only mutually supportive if teachers of both areas have similar philosophies and pedagogic styles. Progressive geography teaching and integrated core humanities have much to offer each other. Geographers should be aware that their skills of spatial analysis and interpretation are important keys to an understanding of the behaviour of individuals, groups, communities and societies, but that this is only one perspective. Working in teams with teachers from other specialist areas can be rewarding and stimulating for students *and* staff.

Notes

1 BEDDIS, R (1983) 'Geographical education since 1960: A personal view' in HUCKLE, J (Ed) *Geographical Education: Reflection and Action*, Oxford, Oxford University Press

2 ROYAL GEOGRAPHICAL SOCIETY (1874) memorandum to the vice-chancellors of Oxford and Cambridge universities, quoted in FREEMAN, T W (1980) *A History of Modern British Geography*, London, Allen and Unwin

3 Cambridge/EMREB examination regulations for the joint certification in geography

English and Integration: Some Problems of Intent

Jeff Lancaster

Start with a personal note: I have spent the majority of my working life teaching in two schools where core English in the fourth and fifth years is described as being 'integrated' i.e. with integrated humanities. In one the course was known as Humanities; in the other as Liberal Studies. The nomenclature discloses both the similarities and differences which existed in both courses.

Having thus established a non-partisan position in the debate, if there is one, on whether English should be 'integrated' with humanities, I will consider the reasons why English teachers should be thinking of such a move.

What Do We Share?

When in doubt, draw a Venn diagram! Although the following definition is loose, that quality can perhaps allow for qualified acceptance of the following as a statement of aims of English and integrated humanities:

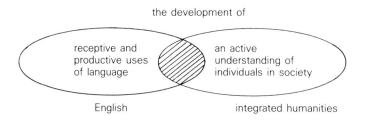

the development of

receptive and productive uses of language

an active understanding of individuals in society

English   integrated humanities

If one looks on literature as language used for and received in specific ways, this definition is not controversially different from the aims for English as set out in the final draft of the *GCSE National Criteria* (aims

1.1.1–3). The definition of the aims of integrated humanities is not dissimilar to the criteria for the selection of topics for inclusion in the MEG integrated humanities syllabus though the definition of aims in that document adds a certain edge to what 'understanding' of society ought to be construed as i.e., understanding socie*ties* involves not only an abstract understanding of 'society' but a personalized understanding of one's own society and others' which would lead to certain attitudes and predispositions, for example, 'a sensitivity and empathy towards people living in other societies', and students' preparation 'for participation in their society'.

That linguistic development and social understanding are in practical ways coterminous is obvious from a consideration of what is necessary for social understanding to develop. Again a look at the *assessment objectives* of the MEG integrated humanities syllabus shows a number of objectives which English teachers, regardless of whether 'integration' were their intention, would probably feel to be part of their province:

> b) the ability to locate, select, extract and record information from a wide range of sources ... and distinguishing that which should count as relevant evidence;
> c) the ability to analyze and interpret information and evaluate arguments ...
> ii) the ability to evaluate the extent to which information, statements and arguments might be biased;
> d) the ability to use information to communicate explanations, ideas and arguments, clearly and coherently through an appropriate medium.

It is clear from these brief quotations that this syllabus, and it is probable all other integrated humanities syllabuses, are *language-demanding*. By this I mean simply that the syllabus demands students who are capable of reading and writing a variety of texts, some, but not all, in the sort of continuous prose which any English syllabus would also demand.

The convergence of English and integrated humanities operates not only at the level of objectives, assessment or otherwise, but also in their declared shared aims. As a belated concession to the 'personal development' lobby the English *GCSE National Criteria* lists as one of its aims:

> The course should seek to develop the ability of students to:
> 1.1.4. understand themselves and others.

— a net so wide it must catch the aims of integrated humanities and many others too!

Integration: The Benefits

So far the discussion of broader integration has been in terms essentially of the overlap between English and integrated humanities, and, to be more explicit, the advantages to an integrated humanities course of having its language demands well provided for. But what are the advantages to those planning an English course of contemplating broader integration? First, the topics or issues of an integrated course provide a secure, some would argue an over-seductive, anchoring device for a course involving language and literature. Although both English departments in which I have taught have perennially complained of the way integration prevents them from doing what they would otherwise do, even having the choice of topics partially taken out of one's hands is an advantage easy to forget. The choice of *topics* to be covered in an English course is ultimately arbitrary, and one can do worse than abandon oneself to a structure on which one can blame all one's shortcomings. Second, the topics of an integrated course do provide a framework which contextualizes language development which otherwise is in danger of becoming a refinement of language for its own sake. This works at the simple level that students talk and write, particularly, on issues which they know something about. For those of us who have taught broader integrated courses, this fact with familiarity like the very wallpaper, becomes difficult to see but it is nevertheless vital to remind oneself of it.

Such contextualization operates not only at the level of individual tasks but also in the whole range of students' language development. The context works as a content because it allows students to see connections between varieties of language use. It is in fact *Language in Use* with meat on the bones of linguistic repertoire. Whatever limitations there may be for the claims that the right tasks produce spontaneous and sustained language development, there is no doubt that it helps a great deal, and an integrated course carefully planned and updated can provide a framework which produces such tasks.

The reverberations between the various language arts within the field established by an integrated course show best in the quality of individual pieces and in the links, conceptual and linguistic, which students make between them. The position of literature is the most difficult area to deal with, but those seeking particular kinds of outcomes from literature teaching will find integration not only palatable but desirable. However to do so, one probably has to have a conception of the value of reading literature which encourages the making of connections between books and their societies. If one subscribes to that positivistic, degutted conception of what literature is which is behind the majority of present 16+ literature examinations, integration is anathema. But that is only a problem if one sees literature in a way which ignores the social context both of its production and its reception.

The corollary of course is that a particular kind of literature teaching is manifestly encouraged by integration. The use of literary texts in an integrated course can take away the stultifying aura of the 'canon of literature' by placing them in a context of other uses of language. This placing can produce a demystification of literature. Instead of being marginalized as arcane experience fit only for the linguistically adept and spiritually responsive, it returns to what it is — words on a page written by women and men whose place in society is as firmly rooted as is that of the writers of political speeches or instructions on how to repair a broken deckchair.

However, the superficial similarities between the aims and objectives of English and integrated humanities teachers disguise some underlying differences in their intentions and ideological underpinning which have to be faced rather than shied away from: though it might be argued that the differences are more exactly between certain approaches to English teaching and certain approaches to *social studies* teaching which it is the historic role of integrated humanities to dissolve.

English and Integrated Humanities: The Obvious Differences in Objectives

If English and integrated humanities were really as similar as the partial view above might suggest then they would not exist as separate school subjects. So, what is it that exists in their separate syllabi which would not exist in syllabi planned in concert? I would suggest the following list, though it is not meant to be exhaustive.

An English course would not contain, or would lay less emphasis on:

(i) reference to the range of practices loosely describable as 'social science' or 'social studies' methodology, such as survey and interview techniques, and statistical analysis;

(ii) terms and concepts derived from 'social science';

(iii) the reading and writing of non-prose texts, for example statistics and diagrams. (Though even here the English *GCSE National Criteria* suggest a widening of the scope of texts normally used for comprehension: *The course should seek to develop the ability of students to: 1.1.2. understand and respond imaginatively to what they hear, read and experience in a variety of media*.)

One hopes that this is meant to include the sort of non-continuous information prose and sources of information other than writing which integrated humanities courses would wish to use.

I shall restrict the list of what an English course would include which an integrated humanities course would not to two items:

(i) the reading of literature;
(ii) the writing of (non-information) prose.

In fact the list is only a single item — literature. A teacher who does not consider the products of schoolchildren as 'literature' has little chance of successfully teaching English integrated with humanities — or otherwise for that matter.

English and Social Studies: A Conflict of Ideologies

The mutual attraction of English and social studies as school subjects can partly be explained by the fact that they are both interested in the same common ground — human nature or human experience, which for the moment I shall treat as the same thing. The emphasis in social studies is on *understanding*, which includes generalizations, abstraction, prediction and involvement in the world of public policy. The emphasis in English is on *experience*, on the reliving of private lives, on their specificity and idiosyncracy, on a grasping of the particular which may or may not provide a basis for generalization but which must in the first instance be grasped as fully as possible, by intellect and intuition.

A problem is that the 'common ground' can disguise the differences between why the two sides wish to inhabit it, what they are attempting to do on it, and what they are using it for. Social studies and English as separate subjects approach this common ground in different ways, and there is a tendency for both subjects to claim priority for their individual viewpoints and ideologies. This competition is not entirely removed when integration is attempted. We are dealing with a game of 'paper wraps stone, stone blunts scissors, scissors cut paper', but with only two protagonists. At its worst English as a separate subject insists on the individual, irreducible, undetermined stone, and social studies wraps with its all-enveloping and explanatory paper a stone which it then cannot see.

At the core, both disciplines are concerned with what it is to be human. Historically they have, however, come up with different answers which far from providing a ready-made synthesis are held in tension as in a triangle of forces. The disciplines are centrally divided by their approach to the relationship between the individual and society. The focus of English teaching is the individual. A valuation is placed on understanding and empathy with the individual and the private. This shows itself in both the receptive and productive modes of language i.e., what one values in the act of reading and writing. For social studies teachers the emphasis is necessarily on the social as well as the individual. What is valued is insight into the external factors which influence human experience, and this valuation leads to an emphasis on generalizations about groups, and the conditions under which such generalizations can be sustained and verified.

At the risk of being accused of characterizing all English teachers as prone to romantic individualism, and all social studies teachers to a concern only with externality, I set forward the following stereotypes of English and social studies teachers' approaches to this key issue, of individuals and society (table 1).

TABLE 1

Social studies	English
(i) private domain seen as *one* domain: public domain probably seen as more important	private domain seen as primary
(ii) interiority seen as one of the possible means of coming to an understanding of human and social experience	interiority seen as an elusive object whose apperception is difficult enough to achieve without the pressures of 'teleological overlay'
(iii) private domain needs to be located within a social studies framework whose intention is not only to describe but to *explain* human experience	private domain seen as perceptible, but not 'explicable'
(iv) relating of individuality to society, by means of generalization seen as important	expression and perception of its specificity seen as vital

'Interiority' is clearly the central concept here, and is the cornerstone in an ideology, which the opposing ideology would itself attempt to explain. I mean by it the specific nature of lived experience, experienced by individuals both as the raw materials of thier lives, and as a defining factor of their identities.

To summarize — at the risk of complete polarization:

	English	Social studies
Abstract object of interest	human experience	human nature
Focus of attention	individuality	society
Privileged domain	private	public
Mode of description	subjective	objective
Mode of apprehension	intuitive	rational
Form of evidence	specificity	generalization
High valuation	interiority	externality

The valuation of 'interiority' by English teachers is a problem for social studies teachers because:

(i) the phenomenon and the ideology which lies behind it *itself* needs to be explained as a social phenomenon;

(ii) texts which focus on private experience are accepted in some sense uncritically by English teachers as powerful and authentic sources of information, but because of those very qualities provide problems of reliability as social documentation.

Although not usually made explicit in quite this way, I feel that these dichotomies are not complete falsifications of the underlying positions of many of the teachers with whom I have worked in 'integrated' courses. Socialization into separate subject disciplines is a powerful force to overcome, assuming that the issue is merely one of socialization, which I think it is not. The dichotomies produce day-to-day as well as longer-term tensions between teachers of an 'integrated' course who ultimately owe their allegiance to separate subject departments. It is in the teaching of literature that these tensions perhaps become most clearly marked.

It would be a plain untruth not to admit that the teaching of literature provides the English teachers with whom I have worked the greatest cause for concern within integrated courses. Perhaps the reasons can again be exemplified by a series of dichotomies, relating to the approach of social studies and English teachers to literature (table 2).

Integration: The Dangers

At its worst literature in an integrated course is chosen to fill necessary gaps in a topic. A poem apparently on an environmental issue is taught

TABLE 2

'Social studies' approach	'English' approach
Selection of literary texts based on light which can be thrown on a particular topic, concept, issue	based on a variety of criteria, one of which may be a loosely defined 'quality'
tendency to focus therefore on literature with a manifest social content — at worst selection of texts which concentrate on their social content in opposition to their literary value.	or as an example of a particular 'genre'
Use of texts 'reading' of literature predisposed towards limited set of acceptable 'readings' or ends which are predetermined when understanding of society becomes foregrounded in the act of reading foreclosing the openness of interaction between text and reader	(i) open-ended search for pattern and meaning within text. Result — interaction of text, teacher and students determines the outcome of of the learning experience; (ii) often text chosen for *formal* rather than contentual properties, for example, control of climax, characterization. The relevance of formal properties and understanding of 'genre' is considered by many to be extremely complex, and problematically connected with an overt understanding of society

because the topic is the environment, with too little attention paid to the fact that what is most interesting about the poem is its formal properties, and not its overt content, which may in any case be of minor importance for its overall meaning. Not any old poem on dead fish and frothy water will do!

The premature foreclosing of the search for meaning in a text, once overt social content has been grasped, and on the other hand the socially-irresponsible exam-focussed revelling in structure and sound are the opposite ends of a continuum. In my experience there is a tendency amongst English teachers in an integrated course to move toward the latter position, with occasional symptoms of guilt about the relevance to the unit later.

The last decade has produced a great complexity of critical approaches to literature, notably structuralism and its associated later developments. There is a job to be done in translating the theoretical insights of modern sophisticated marxist literary theory into classroom practice, and this may point toward the resolution of these pangs of guilt. That the social relevance of literature be limited to its manifest content and the social context of its means of production, is the hangover from a crude reflectionist position in marxist literary theory in any case. The road to 'social relevance' is more complex than through the class membership of the author or hero. Present developments in literary theory point to a variety of ways in which literature can be socially located. It is one of the tasks of those English teachers involved in integration to think through more clearly than heretofore the place and purpose of literature teaching in such courses.

The second tension which I would wish to highlight for English teachers in an integrated course is the possible underestimation by social studies (*and* English teachers for that matter) of the language demands of material included in the course for reasons of its content. Although this can be seen in *reading* material which is simply too difficult for most students, being chosen for the light it throws on issues, its effect is probably more pernicious, because less obvious, in the case of *writing*. There is little point in asking most students to write in a difficult linguistic 'register', particularly that of formal, official prose for two reasons:

(i) if the register matters as much as the content, what do you do if it is not achieved?
(ii) if the register does not matter, why ask for it in the first place?

The latter case is one where the linguistic demands were probably underestimated. The former case leads to my final point on the dangers of integration: when does the English get taught? It is a difficult job to teach children to read the write, so difficult that most schools invent a separate subject to do that, and other things, and call it 'English'. What tends to happen in integrated courses is that the specifics of language development tend to be overlooked. I would argue that there are two reasons for this. First, a simple misunderstanding of how complex teaching language is. Second the difficulty of designing what I have learned to call a 'matrix' of English objectives which will fit over the 'matrix' of an integrated humanities course in such a way that one is left with an integrated course at all.

In some circumstances it may be possible to avoid this problem. Those circumstances rely on language being acquired automatically as part of the wider course. In retrospect I would probably say that these circumstances arise only when the teachers involved are good enough at this kind of understated teaching of language, and when enough students are capable of learning language in such a way. In other circumstances it is probably necessary to design activities specifically intended to produce language learning. This *cannot*, in an integrated content mean a separate English course, else where is one's integration? But it can mean a systematic approach to the learning of language, and this in turn means the acceptance that language is not merely *acquired*, but in some instances — probably for most students — needs to be *consciously* acquired, with the active help of the teacher.

Integration of English in Humanities: The Preconditions

If the dichotomies between English and social studies referred to earlier are not mere chimera, then the preconditions for integration are twofold:

(i) The differences in approach between English and social studies as disciplines and in the approach of their respective teachers must be realized, and faced up to. Rather a realization that opposition is true friendship than a simmering resentment based on the denial of differences. In concrete terms this means teaching those aspects of English and social studies which are thought valuable in an integrated course to the limits, without attempting to smooth away the difficult edges of, say, research technique or poetic appreciation. What we do not want is an 'integration' which denies the validity of insights which are dissonant rather than easily compatible. Real meat and fresh vegetables, not a mixture which offends vegetarians and the palate alike!

(ii) The second precondition is more important. An integrated course must *not* be a casuistic sewing together of social studies and English with the occasional agreement to differ, but a truly *integrated humanities* course. To be a humanities course at all it must approach what I have described as 'interiority' with a full seriousness, not shying away from the difficulties of reconciling the texture of private experience, and the features which shape the experience. In particular it means an integrated course where literature is valued as a unique insight into the lives of ordinary people related to the society from which it arises, and capable of elucidating the *specifics* of that society to members of another in a mediated but powerful way. In the interstices of determination lies a force which at the moment of its creation is experienced as *free*, and it is that freedom which must be recognized as part of one's understanding of what it means to be human, as much as the external factors which shape experience.

So integrated humanities, whether it is integrated with English or not, must take account of two major ways in which that freedom is expressed: (i) the reading of the writing of others; and (ii) in that act of creative use of language (both talk and writing) which connects all students with literary artists. Language is one of the defining features of humanity, and creativity is one of the defining features of the use of language. *In summary, in an integrated course social studies teaching must become transformed into integrated humanities teaching just as much as English teaching is.*

Organizational Conditions for Integration

So, under what conditions might English and integrated humanities look for a successful integration? To some extent this depends on the stage of secondary schooling at which the integration is envisaged. The nearer to, now, GCSE one is, the more exacting the pressures from each 'subject' to make sure that its own requirements are being met. On the other hand, it surely seems suspicious, at least, that subjects which are separate in the first three years of an all-through secondary school should become integrated — or that integration, while being satisfactory for the early years, becomes undesirable later.

So, a few criteria:

(i) Integrated courses demand integrated planning. You cannot produce an integrated course by tacking English onto a social studies framework. The best that this can produce is a hybrid, at worst a rather creaky federation.

(ii) If a school is serious about integration its structure will reflect it:

(a) two heads of department with responsibility for separate subject discipline courses cannot moonlight as integrated course leaders;

(b) staff who teach the integrated course should do so as a large part of their timetable. It is important that staff involved in integrated courses are socialized into their role as teachers of such courses, and this is unlikely to happen when the courses represent less than half of their timetable.

Both 'integrated' courses in which I have been involved have derived their structure from topics or units which were part and parcel of the integrated humanities syllabus design of the time, for example, the family, education, work, law and order, war and peace. This accords a primacy to a sort of 'content' for integrated humanities which is now being questioned. A more broadly integrated course may need to preserve some aspects of such issues or topics but at the same time accord an importance to units which one might find in a separate English course, such as the comedy, representation, speech and writing to be found in different cultures. Too much of the reality of previous courses which integrated English has been a willing attempt by English teachers to build language and literature teaching into a previously decided framework of *social studies* units. The way forward, and the *only* one as I see it, is that teachers should also attempt to build units whose starting point is, for example, the tradition of detective or mystery story writing or oral culture.

Ultimately, too, for a course to be integrated its forms of assessment must not perpetuate the assessments relevant to separate subjects. One of the effects of GCSE has been to make more rather than less difficult any real consideration of what integrated assessment schemes could be.

The Case for Integration

This article's argument has throughout, quite deliberately, been made in terms of a consideration of English and humanities (sometimes 'social studies') as separate subjects. To continue for just a little longer along this track one of the prerequisites of an integration of English with humanities is that neither subject seen in isolation suffers because of the integration. The aspects of what are recognizably 'English' or 'humanities' must be taught as well as if they are taught separately. One and one must, at rock bottom, make at least two. It may, with a little conceptual juggling, be possible to design a course with this idea in mind, but such a design is likely to produce what I would call a 'federation' or at best an 'unstable hybrid' likely to revert to its separate genes in the first or second generation.

The only real reason for seeking integration is that — and the metaphor falls apart in one's hand at this point — one and one make at least three. On the occasions when integration of English and humanities works, it produces understanding of a kind qualitatively different from either English *or* humanities in isolation, and if there is a real case for integration it must in the end lie in that different kind of outcome. At its best integration produces students whose insights into the connection between different ideas, and different forms of language outstrip the understanding of those who teach them, students who move along the seamless web of language and thought forging links between the insight a poem gives, and statistics on the distribution of wealth and income. That any formal education they later receive is likely to resocialize them into the mores of separate disciplines is testament to the conservatism of most higher education courses, and the difficulty of systemizing a practice whose strength lies to a great extent in its spontaneity and evanescent unities. At some stage there will be only one study, the study of community of humans, but, if I remember right, that stage is after the revolution, and we are left with the problem of what to do in the meantime.

The Integrated Humanities Association: Some Recent History

Deirdre Smith

From the foregoing articles it can be seen that for a variety of reasons there is now a substantial and growing body of experience in integrated humanities. Since most of the experience reported is from one area, Leicestershire, it needs stressing that there is now a nationwide movement towards the inclusion of integrated humanities courses in the school curriculum. Under these circumstances the need for a national association which would address itself to the aims of clarifying the issues, providing support to teachers involved in the introduction or reappraisal of courses, and coordinating and disseminating information on developments in integrated humanities, has clearly emerged.

The national Integrated Humanities Association had its inception at a one-day conference in London, in November 1983, convened by members of the Leicester-based Coordinating Committee for Integrated Humanities and the Southern-based Humanities Working Party. This first conference identified the truly national nature of the movement and the first committee meeting in March 1984 was attended by representatives of regional groups from the North-West, the East and West Midlands, South Midlands/East Anglia, the South-West, the Greater London area, and Wales. At this meeting the aims of the infant association were formulated and plans for the inaugural national conference to be held at Stantonbury Campus, Milton Keynes, in October 1984, were evolved. So far, developments in integrated humanities had taken place with groups operating in regional isolation and it had emerged that many teachers who wished to set up integrated humanities courses felt isolated within their own schools. The Association, it was agreed, would:

(i) foster links between teachers and between regional groups, and encourage and help coordinate local and regional initiatives;

(ii) provide a forum for discussion on the nature of integrated humanities in secondary schools;

(iii) promote integrated 'core' humanities as a positive response to the current re-appraisal of the 14–16 curriculum;

(iv) disseminate information on schemes which embody the principles of integrated humanities, and in particular, those which have been submitted to the 16+ examining groups.

In initial fulfilment of these aims the committee members took it upon themselves to circulate as widely as possibly within their regions, membership forms and details of the new Association, and of the forthcoming conference. All new members received copies of the syllabi in 'humanities' submitted to the Southern Regional Examining Group and the 'integrated humanities' submitted to the Midlands Regional Examining Group. The conference was seen as the most immediate step towards fulfilment of aims (ii) and (iii) above.

The response to the initial membership drive and to the inaugural conference was a clear endorsement of the need for such an association. It should be noted that, from the beginning this had been a development derived from a 'grass-roots' model where enthusiastic teachers had taken pupil needs and the learning process as their starting point. Membership and conference charges were accordingly kept to the minimum so that there could be maximum representation of teachers in this category. To date the movement has received no formal DES or other external funding and its existence derives from the enthusiasm and commitment of its members and their conviction of the need to provide a supportive association for current developments in integrated humanities, and a forum whereby the practice of its members may become both informed and strengthened.

The 1984 conference at Milton Keynes was a great success, despite the fact that uncertainties created by the possibility of industrial action at this time had caused delays in the dissemination of conference literature. The wide selection of workshops were run, in the main, by practising classroom teachers of integrated humanities although guest speakers included Maurice Holt on 'integrated humanities, prospects and opportunities' and Daniel Chandler on 'computers and literacy'. Maurice Holt urged that now was the time to exploit the notion of humanities, and that subject knowledge should be used to develop areas of enquiry which relate to issues and so bring subject teachers' expertise into sharp focus on these issues. He believed, with Aristotle, that human beings should work to live, rather than live to work and that the teaching of humanities would help us to do this. He argued that ultimately our task is to let pupils find out that all questions of fact actually have value judgments implicit in them, and so we must help our students develop a capacity for judgment. Daniel Chandler urged teachers of humanities to hijack the computer as a 'subversive device', and reminded us of McLuhan's words that we are all robots unless we critically involve ourselves with our technologies. Roy Nevitt's drama group very effectively showed the potential of theatre-in-education for humanities teachers. Their plays were based on oral material collected from local inhabitants as part of their 'living archives' project.

Course participants chose from a number of practical workshops which included:

Creating a humanities course 11–14
Creating a humanities course 14–16
Team planning and resourcing 11–14
Team planning and resourcing 14–16
The relationship of single subjects to humanities
Experiential learning in the classroom
Experiential learning out of school
Community action
Contentious issues — peace education
                            multicultural education
                            learning for community change

Representatives from the Northern, Midland and Southern Examining Groups reported on the development of 16+ working parties in integrated humanities. It was noted that national criteria had not yet been established for the humanities and it was generally considered that it should be a future responsibility of the Association to provide some response. Retrospectively it is clear that integrated humanities syllabi will be established on the basis of the national 'General Criteria'.

At the Association's AGM held at the conference a new national committee was elected with representatives from each of the areas outlined above. A full list of regional representatives is appended so that readers may determine their nearest local link to the Association. All members and course participants were circulated with this list plus a full list of people attending the course, so that cooperative ventures might be facilitated. At the AGM it was also resolved to explore the possibilities of making links with curriculum development projects such as World Studies; to make contact with English teachers not yet involved in humanities, and to establish links between the IHA and other organizations such as NATE and ATSS. Finally, the success of the conference was marked by numerous requests for further conferences and although the possibility of further weekend conferences seemed unlikely the Committee agreed to stage two further one-day conferences during the 1984–85 school year. Attendance at the conference had far exceeded expectations, and it was evident that morale was high, the membership optimistic, and that with such support the Integrated Humanities Association had indeed become a going concern. Full reports on a number of these workshops are available from Harvey Monte, IHA Newsletter Editor and Information Officer. Several of these are fairly substantial documents and contain detailed advice on curriculum development. Anyone interested can obtain them, cost 50p plus 20p postage, from Harvey at the ILEA History and Social Science Teachers' Centre in Clapham.

The one-day conferences were planned for March 1985 and were to take place in London and Doncaster with the intention of providing a northern and southern venue in accordance with the national dimension the Association had now gained. Members had suggested that workshops might be structured to cater for the varying experience in integrated humanities of the members. Accordingly we planned for three morning workshops on the theme 'Organization and management of an integrated humanities department' with options provided as follows:

   (i) biased towards departments formed from history, geography and RE and people who have worked for several years in integrated situations;

   (ii) biased towards departments formed from a wider range of subjects, and people who are new to integrated humanities;

   (iii) for those setting up, or established in integrated humanities, for the 14–16 age group.

The afternoon session was planned to offer workshops on the theme: 'Key approaches to effective "integrated" teaching'. The options within this session were to include any two from the following:

   (i) Talking;

   (ii) Streetwork;

   (iii) Humanities for a changing lifestyle;

   (iv) Global issues in the humanities;

   (v) Humanities and multiracial education.

The final session was to include for all participants a discussion regarding the introduction of GCSE national criteria. All of these workshops were planned in accordance with the perceived needs of the Association's membership, and all were seen as meeting present concerns.

In the event we were finally unable to stage either conference due to members' response to the industrial action which dominated most of 1985. Like other professional organizations the Integrated Humanities Association cannot thrive in a climate created by falling teacher morale as a result of threats to pay and conditions of service. The Association relies on the active commitment of its members to the development of the learning process. Under these circumstances the kind of support we seek to offer is difficult to deliver. Teachers of integrated humanities are seeking support for curriculum development but the overwhelming feeling of the Committee has been that this is an inappropriate time to hold national conferences until the present dilemma is resolved. We will offer these conferences again when a conclusion to the industrial action has been reached.

In the meantime it would be most disappointing if the early initiatives, so founded on the needs of teachers, were to become dissipated through lack of coherent action. The Committee has no intention of allowing this to happen. Given the prevailing circumstances a further positive initiative has been made by the Committee, entailing the setting up of a *resources exchange* as part of our services to members. The latest newsletter has contained details of our keenness to:

   (i) compile lists of resources which teachers have found of particular value both in preparing their own resources and in direct use with pupils;

  (ii) create a system for the exchange of ideas, whether at the level of planning whole courses, or for individual lessons;

 (iii) consider the publication of an occasional paper/journal if members indicate their willingness to contribute by providing an article, or some lesson notes to the Information Exchange.

Paul Archer, a Committee member who is an advisory teacher at the Urban Base, Bordesley Centre, Birmingham, has volunteered to coordinate the resources exchange. Everything here will depend, of course, on the willingness of members to contribute to the exchange, and on the promotion of membership to the IHA, since financing of the scheme will involve us in considerable additional expenditure. It should, however, provide an invaluable service to all those interested in the introduction or development of integrated humanities courses, and we would hope to offer this as a permanent contribution to services offered to the membership by the IHA. At least we hope that the provision of this service will play an important part in supporting the motivation and enthusiasm of the Association's membership in these difficult times.

Our most recent concerns have been with the needs of members for information on curricular developments and those who have renewed membership will have received the current edition of 'CLIO', ILEA's journal for London teachers of history and social sciences, which is a special edition dealing directly with developments in integrated humanities throughout the country. Many of the contributors to this journal have also been directly involved in the committee work of the IHA. At the time of going to press the Association is hoping to organize a national conference of local authority humanities advisers and HMI interested in integrated approaches.

Recent publicity information for the IHA has included the following statement:

How is 'Integrated Humanities' Being Defined?

Humanities is seen as referring to a core area of study in secondary schools which has to do with people — whether considered as individuals, groups, communities, societies or a species sharing common characteristics and inhabiting the planet earth. 'Integration' is seen as referring to an approach through themes rather than conventional academic disciplines, but making use of concepts and methodologies drawn from a wide range of such disciplines — including those not usually encountered at secondary school level — and concerned to employ methods of learning which are often common to a wide range of humanities studies. It also implies an approach that seeks to develop skills rather than simply inculcating information; for example, the ability to frame aspects of social experience as issues for investigation, to search for and select information from various sources, to explore the meaning of the evidence through discussion, writing and other forms, and to present ideas, explanations and arguments in a range of media. Much of this draws not only on techniques of social research but also on language uses typically promoted by English as a school subject, both language for arriving at a viewpoint and language for communicating it. The importance of direct experience in 'integrated humanities' constitutes another link between social studies and English, and also with moral education.

However, integrated humanities is not seen as necessarily replacing any of the existing school subjects. As a 'core offering' it employs both the techniques and the teachers of a range of subjects which continue to be offered separately in the curriculum to a greater or lesser degree. It does, however, make claims on the support of a major section of the teachers in the humanities area of the curriculum and it is seen as a serious part of the work of all students in a school. For this reason an important question facing all concerned is the manner of its examination at school leaving age. For integrated humanities to be taken seriously as part of the common core of secondary school curriculum it must be capable of public assessment at 16. The most sensible way of doing this would rely mainly on school based continuous assessment over the final two years of the secondary school.

Why is the Association Coming into Existence Now?

Because
(a) the 16+ examining groups for GCSE in the Northern, Midlands and Southern areas all now have integrated humanities syllabi which embody the general principles mentioned above and these syllabi deserve widespread support;
(b) the situation of falling rolls and contracting staffing calls for fundamental reappraisal of current curriculum;
(c) public disquiet has been expressed across the political spectrum with the relevance of conventional approaches for the majority of young people in schools. It is important that teachers take note of this disquiet and respond in well-considered, professional ways — otherwise ill-considered, non-educational solutions could be imposed. A growing number of teachers see integrated 'core' humanities as one such positive response.'

In the same way as integrated humanities is not seen as not necessarily replacing any existing school subjects, the Integrated Humanities Association does not seek to replace any of the existing association loyalties of its members. It is to be hoped that teachers of humanities will perceive the advantages of taking up membership of the IHA whilst retaining their membership of other associations such as GA, HA, ATSS and NATE. It is for this reason that membership subscriptions have been kept to the lowest realistic figure (at the time of going to press £5).

Deirdre Smith

The most recent move towards integrated humanities in schools has in part been due to external pressures: government policies, the impact of TVEI initiatives in local authorities, pragmatic considerations such as the saving in teacher time and improved balance in the curriculum facilitated by integration of traditional subject areas. Although at the outset this was not a major consideration for the Association there is no doubt that such pressures have created a substantial increase in the number of teachers who are looking to an Integrated Humanities Association to provide support for the development of courses more appropriate to the emphasis on the active preparation of the learner for participation in the modern world. Many teachers of traditional subjects within the broad humanities, therefore, look to the IHA for information and support, and it seems likely that this will continue to be an area of growth for the Association. Under these circumstances therefore, the Association may be seen as a nationwide group of teachers, committed to integrated humanities, and to serving the aims of the Association as outlined above.

In a curious way therefore it would seem that pressure from both the core and the periphery of learning in integrated humanities are impelling teachers towards a single goal — the introduction, or rein-forcement, of integrated humanities within the classrooms of the nation. We are finally presented with an opportunity that will allow us to harness the initiatives and expertise of those who have been centrally involved in the evolution of integrated humanities over the past ten years to the needs of classroom teachers who, whatever the motivation, wish to involve themselves in a similar process. From such a merger may come the evolution of a humanities curriculum truly fitted to the late 1980s and 1990s.

Appendix

The Membership Secretary of the Integrated Humanities Association is Nina Wroe, 3 South Brook Cottages, South Brook Lane, Bovey Tracey, Devon. General enquiries relating to the IHA should be forwarded to this address. Enquiries relating specifically to the proposed Resources Exchange should be directed to Paul Archer, 35 Hawthorne Road, Bournville, Birmingham, B30 1EQ.

Regional Coordinators for the IHA:

North West (also Secretary)	David Dickinson, 124 Chesham Road

	Bury, Lancashine, BL9 6EL
London and the South East	Harvey Mante, ILEA History and Social Science Teachers' Centre, 377 Clapham Road London SW9 9BT
South West	Martin Doolan, 25 Westrop, High Worth, Swindon, Wiltshire
North East	John Watson, The Advisers' Centre, 2 The Esplanade, Sunderland
Midlands (also Publicity Officer)	Paul Archer, Urban Base, Bordesley Centre, Camp Hill, Stratford Road, Birmingham
Wales	Steve Smith, 12 Dee Hill Place, Llangollen, Clwyd
South of England	Tony Welch Oaklands School, Lords Hill, Southampton, Hampshire

Notes on Contributors

Gary Coleby was born in London and has taught in Leicestershire for several years, having trained in the humanities group at the University of Leicester School of Education. He is currently involved in a teachers' publishing cooperative, designing resource materials for integrated humanities in particular, while continuing to teach full-time.

Den Corrall is now Deputy Head of a Leicester school serving a largely underprivileged area. Before that he was Head of Humanities at one of the leading Leicestershire community colleges and one which has pioneered integrated humanities as a central element of the curriculum. He is Chief Examiner for the MEG Integrated Humanities syllabus.

Derek Francis is Head of Humanities at a Leicestershire high school (10–14) where he has developed, over the last ten years, an integrated humanities course as a central part of the curriculum throughout the school. He trained in the University of Leicester School of Education humanities group and has recently completed a Master's course there.

Jim Greany is Humanities Convenor at a Leicestershire high school (11–14) with a reputation for well-developed independent learning and team approaches. Earlier he taught at the well-known Thomas Bennet School in Crawley as a member of the Humanities Department there. He has also taught in Papua New Guinea. He has recently completed a Master's degree at the University of Leicester School of Education.

John Haslam is Head of Humanities at a former Leicestershire grammar school, now a 14–18 upper school. Before that he worked in the same Department with Den Corrall, also fully involved in core integrated humanities teaching. He has a Master's degree from the University of Birmingham Centre for Contemporary Cultural Studies.

Viv Keller is Head of Geography and a member of the integrated humanities team at another Leicestershire upper school and community college, having earlier taught at an 11–14 high school. She is currently involved in 16+ experimental syllabi in both integrated humanities and geography.

Lesley King is Head of a Leicestershire High School (11–14), having previously taught integrated humanities in Ealing, Leicestershire and Wiltshire. She did a variety of jobs between leaving school and doing a social science degree at the University of East Anglia followed by training with the humanities group at the University of Leicester School of Education.

Jeff Lancaster is now Head of English in a Clwyd school where English and humanities are integrated in the older years. Before that he also taught with Den Corrall in a Leicestershire integrated humanities course which integrates English. He is an active member of the National Association for Teaching English.

Ross Phillips is currently Acting Deputy Head of the Leicestershire Community College with which several of the other contributors are associated, having been Head of Humanities in succession to Den Corrall. He has also taught English and social science. He originally trained in the humanities group at the University of Leicester School of Education.

Carolyn Robson is currently working at home bringing up children, having been Head of Humanities at a Leicestershire high school (11–14) which had integration as a core area of study. She has a Master's degree in educational studies from the University of Leicester.

Carol Saunders is in her first post and is concerned with a history option course at the same school as Ross Phillips, being also centrally involved with the integrated humanities core. She originally trained at the University of London Institute of Education as a history teacher.

Deirdre Smith is Head of Humanities at a Clwyd school and currently national chairperson of the Integrated Humanities Association. She is involved with history as well as integrated humanities and has been coopted to the Secondary Examinations Council history panel for GCSE criteria.

Viv Styles is Language Support Coordinator at a Wolverhampton school, having been fully involved in the development of integrated humanities at the school. She trained originally at the University of Leicester School of Education in the humanities group.

145

తెలుగు